IN-HOUSE
BOOKBINDING and REPAIR

Sharon McQueen

illustrations by
Ellen Latorraca

additional illustrations by
Richard Douglas Wambold

The Scarecrow Press, Inc.
Lanham, Maryland • Toronto • Oxford
2005

SCARECROW PRESS, INC.

Published in the United States of America
by Scarecrow Press, Inc.
A wholly owned subsidiary of The Rowman & Littlefield Publishing Group, Inc.
4501 Forbes Boulevard, Suite 200, Lanham, Maryland 20706
www.scarecrowpress.com

PO Box 317
Oxford
OX2 9RU, UK

British Library Cataloguing in Publication Information Available

Library of Congress Cataloging-in-Publication Data

McQueen, Sharon, 1961-
    In-house bookbinding and repair / Sharon McQueen.
    p. cm.
    Includes bibliographical references and index.
    ISBN 0-8108-5224-1 (pbk. : alk. paper)
    1. Bookbinding--Repairing--Handbooks, manuals, etc. 2. Books
--Conservation and restoration--Handbooks, manuals, etc. 3. Library
materials--Conservation and restoration--Handbooks, manuals, etc.
I. Title.
Z700.M38 2005
025.7--dc22   2005016080

♾™ The paper used in this publication meets the minimum requirements of
American National Standard for Information Sciences—Permanence of
Paper for Printed Library Materials, ANSI/NISO Z39.48-1992.
Manufactured in the United States of America.

To Richard Douglas,
for his unwavering support and forbearance
S.M.

To Maria Arce and Kazoua Her,
who are steadfast on the front lines of retrieval and repair
E.L.

Contents

Preface

This manual was created for the course Book Repair and Binding taught by James Twomey at the University of Wisconsin–Milwaukee, School of Library and Information Science (now School of Information Studies). James Twomey is the proprietor of Book Preservation Company in Kenosha, Wisconsin, and an adjunct instructor at the School of Information Studies. His course was designed to "prepare the student to set up a simple repair lab and oversee the rebinding and repair of 20th- [and 21st-] century cloth-bound volumes." The course also touched on various aspects of book preservation.

While initially produced as a text for students of library science/studies who may, at some future point in their careers, create and/or supervise a bookbinding and repair lab in a library setting, such a manual as this will prove valuable to librarians in management and administration (all library sizes), individuals interested in private practice, and curious book lovers. The manual was ultimately meant to serve as a basic working document for those who were taking the course or for those who had completed the course and had progressed to professional practice. As such, this guidebook contains both information on setting up the lab (design, equipment, tools, and supplies) and instructions for binding and repairing books. The primary concentration is on the lab setup and the binding process, with common preservation and repair issues frequently encountered during the process mentioned along the way. Repairs are not covered extensively, as many other sources exist (basic as well as advanced) to serve as guides to recognizing these problems and implementing various solutions to them. Some of these sources can be found in a selected bibliography included as an appendix to this manual. Also included are an extensive glossary, resources, and a separate section on World Wide Web resources.

Products and equipment are recommended in sidebars throughout the manual. These products of high quality are produced by reliable manufacturers and are recommendations meant as a starting point only. In most cases, multiple and equally reliable manufacturers can be found to be distributing products of equally high quality. In some cases, the reader may prefer a product other than the one recommended. Experimentation with an assortment of vendors is encouraged.

Before moving forward with any plans for a repair lab, an individual, institution, or organization must conduct a cost-benefit analysis. As appealing as an in-house bookbinding and repair lab may be, other options may prove to be more feasible, cost-effective, or just plain realistic. For example, it may be preferable to send volumes to a commercial bindery. Once the decision to "set up shop" has been made, however, it behooves the individual(s) charged with the planning and implementation of the lab to assure its success. This beginner's manual is designed to assist in that enterprise.

Acknowledgments

This manual primarily owes its existence to the exceptional James Twomey. The author acknowledges the immense debt owed Mr. Twomey for his design and instruction of the first-rate and ever-popular course for which this manual was created.

I am grateful to Barry Annis and Worzalla Publishing Company of Stevens Point, Wisconsin, for their willingness to allow me access to their various book production processes. Tours of Worzalla greatly enhanced my understanding of 20th- and 21st-century cloth-bound books and samples freely and generously given have been enormously useful for practice, study, and teaching purposes. Thanks are also extended to Wisconsin Book Bindery of Milwaukee, Wisconsin, for an enlightening tour and samples shared. I am indebted to David Sarmas of Aabbitt for advice most helpfully offered and to J Spear Associates for many favors.

Publisher and author Gareth Stevens kindly gave a great deal of his time, expertise, and advice, as did Timothy Ericson, university archivist, UW–Milwaukee, Golda Meir Library. Many thanks to them both. Rebecca Hall and Dr. Thomas Walker of UW–Milwaukee, School of Information Studies, have always given support when needed. What wonderful people they are! A hearty thanks is extended to several of my UW–Madison, School of Library and Information Studies doctoral dissertation committee members for allowing me the time away from my dissertation to complete this manual: Dr. Douglas L. Zweizig, Dr. Anne Lundin, Dr. Greg Downey, Kathleen T. Horning, and Dr. Louise Robbins (Chair). SLIS Laboratory Library Director, Dr. Michele Besant, has been troubled by me for every project I've undertaken since her arrival on the job. She is the very soul of library service.

I am obliged to many members of the Scarecrow Press team for their diligence and hard work, including Adrianne Brigido, Sally Craley, Trina Grover, Mary McConnell, Sue Easun, Edward M. Kurdyla, and Martin Dillon. I am especially fortunate to have had an early reading and the comments of an unknown reviewer. The input of this individual greatly improved the manuscript and I am grateful. I consider myself lucky to have retained the talented and thorough indexer, Tana Elias. A very special thanks is extended to Ellen Latorraca for her excellent illustrations. What a pleasure it has been to collaborate with her.

Thanks to Robert and Alice Sauer for their continued support. Thanks to Carol and Milt Flieller—for countless reasons. This project has received a great deal of invaluable assistance from Richard Douglas Wambold. The gratitude I owe him cannot be expressed here.

Part One: Setting Up Shop

Planning for the lab must be done carefully and thoroughly. Initial set-up costs are *expected* to be higher than ongoing operating costs. It is important to keep this in mind. Do not budget on the low side thinking items can be picked up later "along the way." This mentality usually backfires. Now is the time to budget for, and purchase, whatever is needed.

At this stage, noise concerns may also be addressed. With air-conditioners, air filters, humidifiers, and other appliances in operation, the lab can become a noisy place to work. Employers should be aware that issues surrounding these conditions might arise.

1. The Environment

The Space

Optimally, the space will measure between 1,000 and 2,000 square feet. Often these types of labs end up in basements of older buildings. When this is the case, the lab is inevitably sharing space with a boiler. If a boiler is present a wall must be built around it, preferably a firewall. Heat and safety are concerns. Noise issues caused by all existing basement machinery should also be addressed. Staff will be spending many hours of their lives in this area and it needs to be compatible with human occupancy.

Design/Layout

The lab should consist of a large, open room with the major equipment and supplies centrally located. It works well to have a large, sturdy table in the middle of the room with the equipment placed upon it for easy access. Shelving may be placed under this table to keep supplies centrally located as well. Storage should not be an afterthought, but a planned space requirement. Individual workstations are usually situated on the perimeter of the room facing the walls.

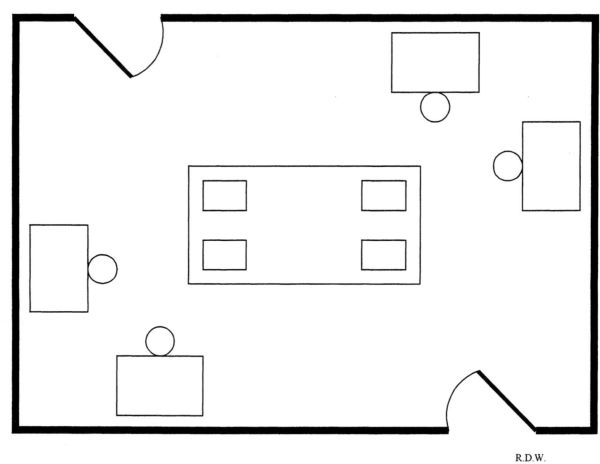

A possible floor plan

Furniture

Table
Centrally located is a large table, sturdy enough to hold the large equipment and other supplies needed by all.

Workstation tables
Each workstation should have a high drafting-type table. Formica tabletops work well for easy cleanup.

Workstation stools
Each workstation should have height-adjustable swivel stools on wheels. Being able to move around easily is very important.

Workstation lamps
Swing-arm lamps with clamps work well to specifically position light.

Shelving
Shelving is necessary to store supplies and hold books (both before and after repair). The shelving should be smooth and free of sharp edges and corners, which can cause damage to books. Steel shelving with a baked enamel finish is preferred. The shelving should be adjustable to accommodate books of different sizes. The bottom shelf should be at least four inches off the floor to allow for air circulation and to prevent damage due to flooding.

Bookends
It is important that books be stored properly, packed neither too loosely nor too tightly.

Electricity

An inspection should be made to determine if the electrical service to the lab needs to be updated and brought up to code. If work is needed, use a reliable contractor and have the work inspected upon completion by the proper municipal authority. A sufficient range is 60 to 100 amps of service, with 60 being an absolute minimum. Space electrical outlets every 6 to 10 feet, so extension cords will not be needed. Each workstation needs its own outlet of at least 60 amps.

Lighting

Ceiling lighting should be fluorescent and consist of 60 watts (four tubes) per 100 square feet. High-quality ballasts will prevent flickering of fluorescent lighting. Ultraviolet light filters (UV filters) should be used to prevent ultraviolet rays from damaging the materials/books. For cellulostic materials, UV light is a kind of poison. It causes chemical reactions which, in turn, cause deterioration.

UV light can be filtered out at its source. Plastic UV filter sleeves may be purchased for fluorescent light tubes and a UV filter film may be applied over any windows to block the UV rays from sunlight. Janitorial staff should be trained in the care and handling of the light tube filters (sleeves). They are not difficult to manage when a light tube needs replacement, but if the staff does not know what they are, they will end up in the trash with the burned-out light tube.

Each workstation should be equipped with individual swing-arm lamps with clamps.

Temperature

It is important that the temperature of the lab be closely monitored. A reliable thermometer is a must. Cooler temperatures are preferred for the preservation of materials—some experts say the colder the better. (It would not be uncommon to find an archival storage area set at 55 degrees Fahrenheit.) The lab, however, is a work environment and therefore comfort of the staff is also a consideration. Of great importance is *consistency* of temperature. For that reason, a level should be selected somewhere between 67 and 72 degrees and should then be maintained. A window air conditioner will do if the building does not have central air (or if the central air does not service the lab area). At least 24,000 BTUs (British thermal units) will be needed. A Sears Kenmore™ is the air conditioner of choice for many. Air conditioners serve as dehumidifiers, as they also remove water from the air.

Humidity

As is the case with temperature, it is important that the humidity of the lab be closely monitored. A reliable hygrometer is a must and a humidifier and/or dehumidifier may be necessary to maintain consistent humidity levels. These devices also circulate air, which helps prohibit mold growth. A humidifier with a 40-pint capacity is adequate.

The lower the humidity, the less likely the lab is to have mold problems. Molds are microscopic organisms that can cause damage to books, documents, and other library materials. They become visible as they grow, spread, and cluster. "Mold" and "mildew" are both forms of fungi and, though differences exist, the terms are often used interchangeably. Mold spores can be found almost everywhere—in almost all outdoor and indoor air. Most surfaces provide enough nutrients for mold to grow. Books and documents are vulnerable, as they are often made of cellulose. In other words, to the mold, they are food. The following conditions are necessary for mold growth:

- Mold spores
- Nutrients/food source
- Moisture/humid conditions
- A temperature range of between 40 and 100 degrees Fahrenheit

In addition to potential mold damage, production rates go down in more humid environments. Glues and adhesives take longer to dry. (It would not be uncommon to find an archival storage area with relative humidity set at 40 percent.) However a humidity level of 50 percent is comfortable for humans *and* cellulastic materials.

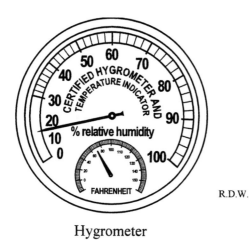

R.D.W.

Hygrometer

A reliable thermometer and hygrometer or a thermohygrometer or hygrothermograph are required. A thermometer measures temperature and a hygrometer measures humidity levels. Many hygrometers come equipped with thermometers (pictured at left).

When a thermometer and a hygrometer are combined in one unit, the instrument is often referred to as a thermohygrometer. A hygrothermograph is an instrument that not only measures, but also records the temperature and relative humidity, along with the date and time. An instrument that provides long-term, continuous recordings of both the temperature and humidity levels in the lab is useful in determining consistency and in discovery of the cause(s) when consistency is lacking.

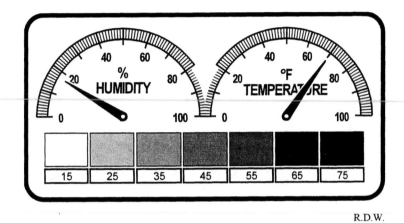

R.D.W.

Thermohygrometer

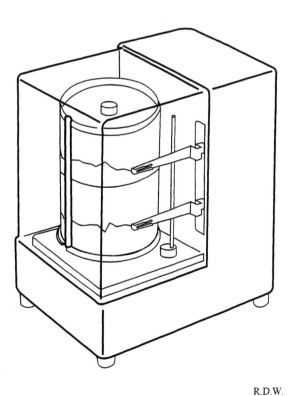

R.D.W.

Hygrothermograph

Air Filtration

HEPA (High Efficiency Particle Arrester) filters remove mold spores and other pollutants from the air. One HEPA filter is needed for every 1,000 square feet. HEPA filters remove particles, down to 3 microns, from the air. To give a sense of size, over 600 microns would fit in the period at the end of this sentence. Mold spores are roughly 10 to 30 microns in size.

Bookbindery and repair labs frequently make use of organic solvents and chemicals, which create fumes that can cause damage to the human central nervous system. In addition, book repair is a dusty business. Workspaces—and lungs—*must* be kept clean. HEPA filters are not an option; they are a necessity. Also, as is the case with humidifiers, they circulate the air, which helps to prohibit mold growth and helps to regulate both temperature and humidity.

HEPA filters can be purchased in several configurations. For lab purposes, the 360-degree type works well. The fan is in the shape of a doughnut and it draws air in from all sides. The air flows through two filters. The first filter (the particulate filter) removes particles from the air. The second filter removes the fumes. HEPA filters have become relatively common and may now be purchased in most hardware and department stores.

Water

A large utility sink is necessary for washing hands and mixing solutions. It must have both hot and cold running water. The water running directly from these taps will not be suitable for many lab purposes. For many lab processes the water must be controlled and as pure as possible. Water will be used as a chemical ingredient and results must be predictable. Two filters will be needed:

Particulate filter
Water often passes through very old systems before it reaches the lab. Particles of rust or sand are commonly found in tap water. A particulate filter removes these particles from the water. A filter that has the capacity to remove down to 5 microns is sufficient. The filter should be changed according to manufacturer instructions.

Activated carbon filter
This filter consists of mesh covered with charcoal. This filter bonds with all carbon molecules, removing organic materials from the water. The filter should be changed according to manufacturer instructions, or every 3 months.

The local yellow pages will provide a list of suppliers, and local photography labs are a good source for recommendations.

2. The Equipment

The specialized equipment discussed in this section tends to be big, heavy, and expensive. On the bright side, these items are onetime purchases. They don't wear out. They outlive you! Many of these items can be purchased used, but the budget must allow for transportation costs. It is not recommended that wooden items, such as the laying press, be purchased used. The wood may be warped or in otherwise poor condition.

Sewing Frame

The sewing frame holds sewing tape taut and holds signatures together as they are sewn into the text block.

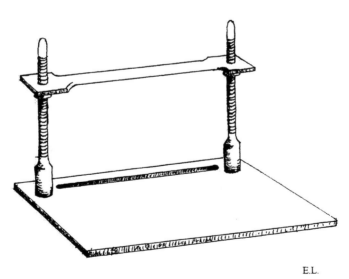

E.L.

Sewing frame

Presses

Presses assist the bookbinder in several ways. Primarily, they are used to put materials under pressure for extended periods of time. This allows sufficient time for drying of adhesives and may also help to give shape to the book. A press may also be used as a "third hand" as the bookbinder works. The pressure is applied either top-down (standing pressure) or side-to-side (laying pressure, also known as "the pinchine effect"). The press and the requirements of the job determine the type of pressure used.

The efficiency (capacity) of a press is measured by its "daylight," which is the maximum amount of space between its platens. The platens are the two surfaces of a press that touch the book when a book (or books) is pressed between them. The more space, the greater number of books a binder can press at once. Daylight affects the price of a press. A press with 30-inch daylight would be considered a good choice, in cost and efficiency, for most labs. A number of smaller units could also be used, rather than one large unit.

A *standing press* applies top-down pressure and usually contains heavy, cast-iron elements.

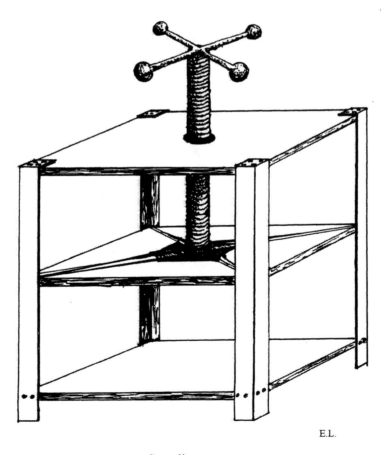

E.L.

Standing press

Standing presses tend to be expensive and alternatives can be used. Two boards, with holes cut into each of the four corners, can serve as the platens. The boards are connected by means of threaded rods, which are used to bring the boards together. Some designs make use of wing nuts, which are screwed down to apply pressure. The boards may be edged with brass, on one edge per each board, to make French joints. (French joints are the grooves at the hinges on the cover of a book.) Also, *press boards* with brass edges may be used with a standing press for the same purpose (see also page 18).

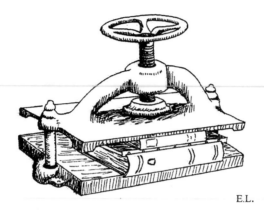

E.L.

Press with a press board placed between two books

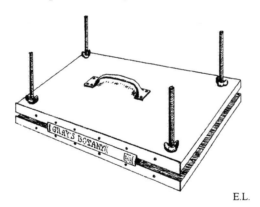

E.L.

Threaded rod press with brass edges and handle

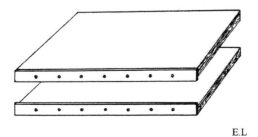

E.L

Press boards with brass edges

A *laying press* or *finishing press* applies side-to-side pressure (laying pressure). It is usually made of wood and is portable. The laying press generally consists of two platens and two large screws. It functions in a manner similar to a vice and holds the book in a sturdy fashion so that it may be worked on (e.g., tooling the title and/or designs onto the spine of the book). The laying press may also be used with two boards to keep books from warping while drying.

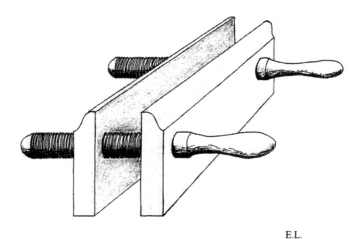

E.L.

Laying press (or finishing press)

E.L.

Job backer (or backing press)

A *job backer* or *backing press* is a type of freestanding laying press. It is often made of cast iron. This type of press, while useful, is not essential.

Board Cutter

Binder's board, a material used in the recasing of books, requires some sort of heavy-duty cutter for proper sizing. While such a cutter consumes substantial lab space and is a major financial invest-ment, it will improve quality and speed. There are two basic types:

Board shears
Board shears are considered the ideal choice. They resemble paper cutters but are much larger, freestanding, and have a curved blade. The blade is self-sharpening and requires little mainte-nance. The blade measures roughly 4 1/2 feet.

Guillotine
A guillotine is usually considerably less expensive than a board shears. Making use of both gravity and applied pressure, the blade falls straight down to cut the board. At least two, if not three blades, should be purchased, as they often need sharpening. Specialty services will pickup and deliver the blades for a reasonable fee. In most cases, a guillotine cannot easily cut more than one board at a time.

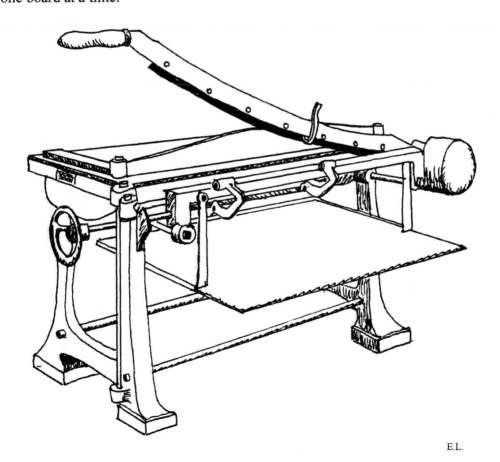

E.L.

Board shears

Hot Foil Stamping Machine

A hot foil stamping machine (also known as a gold foil stamping machine) is a device that heats type and presses it firmly against stamping foil, which in turn presses against the material to be printed. The process impresses information (such as title, author, volume numbers, etc.) onto the front cover and spine of a book. So that the information impressed will be permanent and will not smudge, three factors must be carefully controlled: pressure, temperature, and time. (Some labs use alternative methods of labeling.)

Recommended hot foil stamping machines are manufactured by:

The KWIKPRINT
Manufacturing Company, Inc.
4868 Victor Street
Jacksonville, FL 32207

Toll Free: (800) 940-5945
Local: (904) 737-3755
Fax: (904) 730-0349

Email: kwik@fdn.com

http://www.kwik-print.com

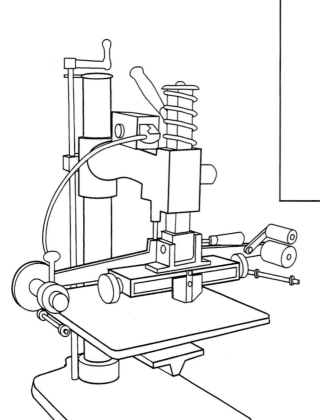

R.D.W.

Hot foil stamping machine

Samples of the various book cloths a lab selects for use may be sent to the hot foil stamping machine manufacturer for application evaluation and testing. This service is usually offered free of charge and is very useful in determining the best foil and book cloth combinations for a particular organization.

The following will be needed for use with a hot foil stamping machine:

Foil
There are three major manufacturers of foil used in the hot foil stamping process: Kurz Transfer Products, ITW Foils, and Crown Roll Leaf, Inc. Foil is not purchased directly from these manufacturers, but from their distributors.

A recommended distributor of foil:

General Roll Leaf Manufacturing Company
10-03 44th Avenue
Long Island City, NY 11101

Toll Free: (888) 868-1876
Local: (718) 784-3737

Email: peterb@generalrollleaf.com

Type
Type is used for the lettering and numbering of books. Type is a onetime purchase, as it wears very little over long periods of time. Most service type is made of zinc, but brass is the premium and therefore, the most expensive. The type size is measured by "points" and there are 72 points to an inch. A standard font and size is 18-point Roman. It would be wise to stock both a larger and a smaller size if budgets permit. A commonly used range for larger books is 24 to 30 point.

A recommended manufacturer of type:

Ernest Schaefer, Inc.
731 Lehigh Avenue
Union, NJ 07083-7626

Local: (908) 964-1280

Both KWIKPRINT and Ernest Schaefer also distribute foil. In addition, KWIKPRINT inventories Ernest Schafer type and Ernest Schafer inventories KWIKPRINT hot foil stamping machines.

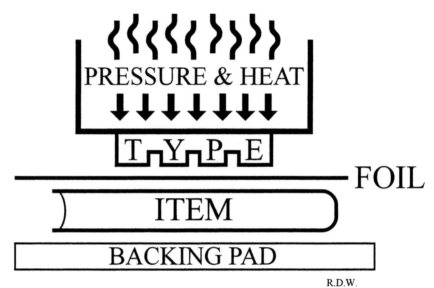

The hot foil printing process

R.D.W.

Hot Plate or Microwave Oven

The lab will stock various adhesives/glues. One of these is starch paste (covered in greater detail in Chapter 4, "The Supplies"). Starch paste must be cooked before it may be used. Either a hot plate or a microwave oven will work for this purpose, though many prefer a hot plate so that the mixture may be more easily watched and stirred. A consistent mixture, without lumps, is desired.

Refrigerator

A small refrigerator is not essential, but is handy for the storage of starch paste. Starch paste spoils more quickly at warmer temperatures and refrigeration can extend its durability. Refrigerator storage helps deter destructive organisms from being attracted by the paste. The type of refrigerators used in college dormitories is sufficient.

Staff should be discouraged from keeping their own food in the lab refrigerator. Food should be kept out of the lab entirely.

3. The Tools

In most cases, tools are an extension of one's hand. They tend to last several years and periodically need replacement. It is a wise move to buy new tools. It generally does not pay, in the long run, to buy them used. They are generally moderately priced, running from 5 to 30 dollars.

Ruler

The ruler is used for measuring and is therefore marked with measurements (ruled). It is important that this tool does not rust, and so it must be made of steel or brass. It must be backed with cork or rubber so it will not slip when in use. Twelve inches is a sufficient length.

Straight Edge

Like the ruler, the straight edge must be made of steel or brass, though it should be longer (18″) and must be thick (1/8″ or greater). The reason for added thickness is that the straight edge is used for cutting. The user does not want the knife blade to jump the edge and possibly inflict injury—to the user or to the book. Proper thickness will help prevent the blade from catching on and riding over the straight-edge or creeping away from the straight-edge, making a bad cut. A 12″ straight edge would be a useful addition to the 18″ for working with smaller books.

Self-healing Mat or Cutting Mat

Commonly available at art supply and office supply stores, self-healing mats are ideal for protecting tabletops during cutting procedures. While not technically a tool, a self-healing mat will prolong the life of some of your tools and equipment (knives and tabletops).

Bags of Lead Shot

Twenty-five pound bags of lead shot conform well to the spine of a book and are useful for applying pressure during drying processes.

Scissors and Shears

The scissors and shears should all be quite sharp. At least three types/sizes are necessary:

- Tiny, very sharp scissors for detailed work
- Regular, medium-sized scissors for cutting paper
- Large, heavy-duty shears for cutting lightweight board and cloth
  (These shears ought to have a blunt end on the bottom blade, like surgical bandage scissors.)

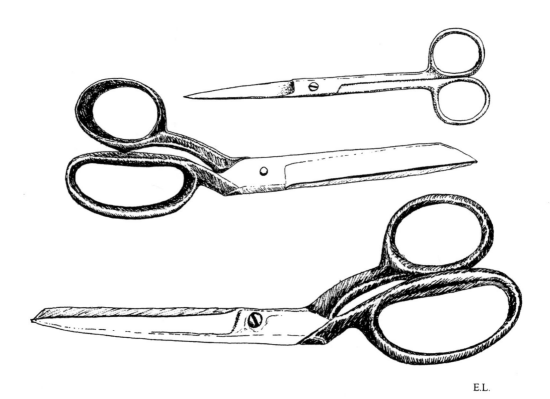

E.L.

Bookbinder's Knives, Surgical Scalpels, or X-Acto™ Knives

Two or three knives of small, medium, and large sizes are desirable (X-Acto™ #11 is the most useful size). It is a good idea to acquire several different handle styles for different cutting jobs. The knives must be very sharp for precise cutting. X-Acto™ knives are an economical alternative to bookbinder's knives or surgical scalpels.

E.L.

X-Acto™ knives

Bone Folder

Bone folders are essentially pieces of cut and polished bone. They are also made of plastic, but those made of bone are comparable in price and are easier to handle (less slippery). In addition, the plastic versions may leave a residue on the material being repaired. This tool is used to fold paper and for shaping during various procedures (e.g., the making of the French groove). A combination tip bone folder is the most useful type. One end of the bone folder should be somewhat rounded and the other somewhat pointed.

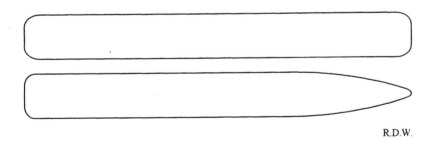

R.D.W.

Bone folders

Tweezers

Often used in conjunction with spatulas, tweezers can assist in lifting and placement procedures.

Spatula

A narrow, stainless steel spatula is a useful tool for many procedures. It is used to lift and remove items, such as old linings and book cloth. It can also be used to apply adhesives. It should be approximately 1/4″ wide with a length of approximately 8″. The spatula should have one pointed end and one that is rounded.

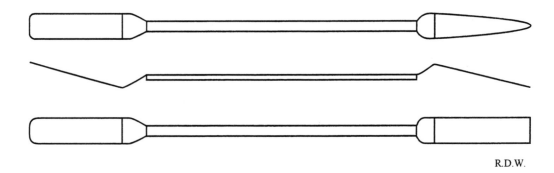

R.D.W.

Spatulas (views from top, side view in center)

Press Boards

The press boards are two pieces of wood with a brass edge screwed onto each one. (Press boards have been previously mentioned in this manual in the section on presses; see page 9.) The brass edge shapes the hinge of the book (French hinge). The press boards and brass edges actually touch the book as it is placed inside a press, helping to shape the book properly. The cover will not remain on the book for long if the book is not formed into its proper shape. Press boards last roughly 5 to 6 years and, at $75 to $100, are the most expensive of the tools.

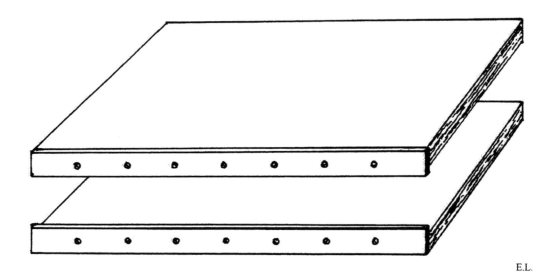

E.L.

Press boards with brass edges

Brushes

The brushes that are most frequently used are primarily used for glue and should be rounded. These sorts of brushes are usually imported and expensive. They are most often made from the hairs of hog's tails, or some other natural material. The ferrule is the band of metal that wraps around the brush. It helps the brush hold its shape and bind the bristles to the head. The ferrule must be non-rusting and so should be made of steel.

It is not a good idea to skimp on these brushes. A good brush should last roughly 7 years if treated correctly, which includes allowing it to dry out between uses. Three sizes of glue brushes are needed:

- Small – 1/4″ to 1/2″
- Medium – 3/4″ to 1″
- Large – 2-1/2″ in diameter

E.L.

Rounded hog's tail glue brush

R.D.W.

Small, nonrounded glue brush

In some cases, it is useful to have a small glue brush that is not rounded, but flat in shape at the ferrule and bristles. A brush with stiff bristles and an unpainted handle is best. In addition, it is helpful to have a dust brush handy to clean off work surfaces.

R.D.W.

Dust brush

Sewing Tools

In the event the text block requires resewing, it will be necessary to employ several tools concurrently with the sewing frame:

Keys
Keys are the objects that hold the cords or sewing tapes to the sewing frame. They must be made of brass or some other metal that will not rust. "A" keys are designed for use with cords. "H" keys are designed for use with sewing tape. It is this latter combination that will be used in this text (see Chapter 4, "Resewing").

Needles
The most useful length for needles is 2-1/2″ long.

Awls
An awl is used to punch holes in the signature, or page(s), when the original holes have been covered by a reinforcing material or if new holes are needed for any other reason.

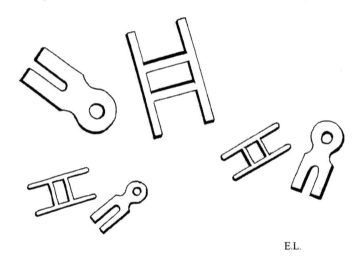

E.L.

Various sewing keys

E.L.

Awl

Hammers

Several types of hammers are useful:

Rounding hammer
The rounding hammer is used to pound the back of the text block into a convex form.

Backing hammer
The backing hammer is used to pound the shoulder into the text block.

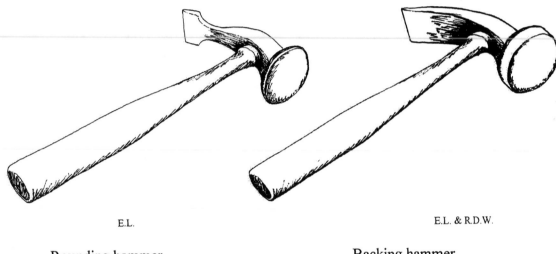

E.L.   E.L. & R.D.W.

Rounding hammer   Backing hammer

Spray Bottle

Several processes entail using an alcohol and water mixture used as a wetting agent (see page 29). A spray bottle works well for the application of the wetting agent to various surfaces.

4. The Supplies

Supplies are consumables that require periodic restocking. They are those items that "get used up" in the book repair process. Keep in mind, most suppliers will send free samples for inspection prior to purchase. Be sure to select materials that conform to current preservation standards.

Adhesives/Glue

There is no all-purpose adhesive, but the lab will be able to function well with just a few types. The most often used are polyvinyl acetate (PVA) and starch paste. There are a few useful terms associated with adhesives:

Setting time
Setting time is the length of time it takes the adhesive to become tacky.

Reversibility
Reversibility is the readiness with which the adhesive can be removed in the future. (The concept of "reversibility" also applies to processes other than adhesive removal.)

Durability
Durability is gauged by the strength and lasting quality of the bond the adhesive creates, and by the length of time it takes the unused portion of adhesive to spoil.

There are several types of adhesives that should be stocked in the lab:

PVA (polyvinyl acetate)/synthetic resins
PVA consists of tiny pieces of plastic suspended in water. As the solvent evaporates, bonding occurs at the molecular level. In other words, as the water dries, the resins form a flexible film.

It is thick and white and has the appearance of Elmer's™ Glue. Each batch of PVA will be of a different consistency. PVA can be thinned with water or thickened by exposure to air.

PVA is the best all-purpose adhesive for lab purposes and it is employed in roughly 95 percent of the procedures. It is inexpensive, pH neutral, has an indefinite shelf life, and is reversible (can be rewet). In addition, synthetic resins are considerably less likely to attract destructive organisms than plant or animal-based adhesives.

A preferred brand of synthetic resin adhesive is Jade 403, made by Aabbitt.

Aabbitt Adhesives
2403 N. Oakley Avenue
Chicago, IL 60647

Toll Free: (800) AABBITT
Local: (773) 227-2700

Email: info@aabbitt.com

http://www.aabbitt.com/

Starch paste
Starch paste is the oldest of these adhesive types. Starch paste is made of vegetable matter, usually wheat, rice, or corn. It comes in powder form. Water must be added and the paste must be cooked before use. Precooked powders can be purchased, which often contain preservatives and/or fungicides. Starch pastes are not "sticky" adhesives and pressure must be applied in order for them to adhere.

After water is added to the powder and a paste is formed, starch paste should be cooked until bubbles form. A hot plate or microwave may be used. The correct consistency will be similar to that of thick cream. After it cools it should be clear. If separation occurs, and the paste becomes "watery," it is no longer useable and should be thrown out.

There are several drawbacks to the use of starch paste. It is a relatively "wet" adhesive and consequently has a relatively long setting time. There is also a durability issue. Once prepared, the mixture is usually serviceable for only one to ten days. The paste spoils more quickly at warmer temperatures and refrigeration can extend its durability. In addition, vegetable matter may attract destructive organisms, such as vermin and insects. Obviously, special care must be taken to avoid these harmful pests. Starch paste tends to be *slightly* alkaline. The benefits of using starch paste are that it is inexpensive, immediately reversible, and close to neutral pH.

Hot melt adhesives

Hot melt adhesives are gaining popularity in some labs. They are 100 percent solids with no wetting agents. The process works by the melting of the adhesive through the application of high temperatures and firm pressure. Upon losing heat, the adhesive returns to its original state, once again becoming a solid. Hot melt adhesives have an indefinite durability relative to their flexibility. The harder the adhesive, the longer it will last. The softer adhesives can lose their strength.

Hide glue

Hide glue is made of animal matter and is not easily reversible. It may be reversed through the use of an enzyme-based solvent. Many older books have traditionally contained this form of adhesive. Conservators are more familiar with this substance than 20th- and 21st-century bookbinders. It is primarily mentioned here because it may have to be dealt with in bookbinding and repair processes. Some labs do make use of hide glue, mainly because its use will allow a book cover to lie exceptionally flat. However, it is difficult to work with in other regards.

Cellulose Gum

Cellulose gum (sodium carboxymethylcellulose or sod. CMC and methyl cellulose or MC) is a thickening agent used to keep a surface moist or for dissolving old adhesive. Adding a small amount to water (3 to 5 percent cellulose gum and 95 to 97 percent water) will produce a solution of "thickened water." When applied to a surface it will "stay put," allowing surfaces to remain moist so that they may be manipulated as needed. It may also be added to PVA to increase the setting time of the PVA when the air is dry. When cellulose gum comes into contact with hide glue an enzyme action occurs, which assists in the dissolving of the hide glue.

Book Cloth

The material used as a covering for book casings is woven fabric, which has been filled in, coated, or painted with acrylic or starch. This coating prevents adhesives from oozing through the fabric. Acrylic-coated cloth is harder to work with but is waterproof, which provides obvious benefits. Starch-coated cloth is not waterproof, but is considerably easier to work with when moistened. Once again, it is wise to remember that starch may attract destructive organisms. A paper-lined book cloth also exists, which makes adhesion to binder's board easier. However, this product is not known to be highly durable.

The durability of book cloth is gauged by the processing of the cloth and the thickness of the thread. The thread thickness determines the *grade* of the book cloth. The grade scale runs from A to G, with A being the thinnest thread and G being the thickest. In selecting a grade of book cloth, staff must consider what type of use the book will be expected to endure and the lasting value of the information contained in the book. C is the thinnest grade that should be used for most jobs. D is the thickest starch-filled grade available and is a good choice for many jobs. F is similar to canvas and, when acrylic-filled, is virtually indestructible. Any book cloth above a C or D grade is called a *buckram*.

Some consideration should be given to the color of the book cloth. Choose colors that are less likely to show dirt and that "age gracefully." In other words, a trendy color may make a fun selection *this* year, but consider how long the book is likely to remain in use. For continuity, it is helpful to keep records of color choices for books bound in a series.

A recommended supplier of book cloth:

ICG Holliston
P.O. Box 478
Kingsport, TN 37662

Toll Free: (800) 251-0451

http://www.icgholliston.com

Hinge Cloth

Every book has, or *ought* to have, a hinge cloth. This is the reinforcing material that, along with the paper endsheets, holds the hard cover onto the text block. The thickness of the thread is not as important a consideration as the tightness of the weave in determining strength for this reinforcement purpose. The stronger the hinge cloth, the better. Cambric and jaconette are fabrics that make good hinge cloth. They are lightweight, tightly woven, and usually lightly sized.

Headband Cloth

Headband cloth is the decorative (usually multicolored) strip of cloth that is applied to the top and bottom of the spine beneath the casing. It is *purely* decorative and has no function.

Binder's Board

The material that provides rigidity to a hardcover book is called "binder's board." When serving as a component of a book's case (what most laypersons refer to as the book's "cover") it is usually covered with some type of book cloth. Binder's board is often made of recycled (inexpensive) paper. As a result, the transportation of the board is more costly than the board itself. If space allows, purchasing by the ton is by far the most economical choice. The boards are usually purchased by the bundle, with seventeen sheets to the a bundle.

Selecting the appropriate thickness of the binder's board is important in the recasing of a book. Using a board thicker than the height of the shoulder will cause the book cloth to tear. The three standard calipers (or thickness measurements) that a lab should have on hand are:

- Thin   .060"
- Medium   .080"
- Thick   .100"

A recommended supplier of binder's board:

Gane Brothers & Lane
Midwest Region (Corporate Offices)
1400 Greenleaf Avenue
Elk Grove Village, IL 60007

Toll Free: (800) 323-0596
Fax: (800) 784-2464

Email: sales@ganebrothers.com

http://www.ganebrothers.com/

Paper

Paper consists of fibers that are bonded together. Various types of paper, used for various purposes, are necessary in the recasing process. When selecting any paper, consider the following:

- Strength and color
- Alkaline paper is preferred as it provides a buffer against future acid contact.
- *Sizing* is an ingredient added to paper as it is being made. Sizing affects water absorption. A wetting agent may be necessary to get the paper to readily accept moisture.
- Regardless of the paper type, it may be desirable to find out if the paper under consideration has passed the Photographic Activity Test (P.A.T.) of the American National Standards Institute, Inc. This is an accelerated aging test that insures the safety of materials used along with photographic materials. Many suppliers will note materials that have passed this test in their catalogs.

Various paper types:

Endpapers (or endsheets)
The endpaper is a thick, folded sheet that is attached to both the casing and the text block. It assists in holding the two together. It also gives the book a "finished" appearance. Endpaper should be strong, thick (60 to 80 lb.), acid-free or alkaline, and usually neutral in color. Off-white is a good color choice, as white is often too stark in appearance.

Dove Gray is an appropriate machine-made paper distributed by Archivart:

Archivart
A Division of Heller & Usdan, Inc.
7 Caesar Place
Moonachie, NJ 07074

Toll Free: (800) 804-8428

Email: sales@archivart.com

http://www.archivart.com

On occasion, a decision may be made to use a handmade (or mold-made) paper for endpapers. Handmade papers of various colors and designs are available and may be used for books of greater value or to more closely approximate a book's original appearance.

Blotter paper
This paper is used during the *casing in* process and may be reused as long as it remains clean.

Lining paper
Handmade paper makes ideal lining paper. Many handmade papers contain long fibers, which make the papers strong. They also often do not contain sizing and as a result, handmade papers are more flexible.

Remember, when folding paper it is best to fold it *with* the grain.

Stamping Foil

Foil is a supply that is needed for use in conjunction with a hot foil stamping machine (see Chapter 2, "The Equipment").

Wetting Agent

Alcohol and water are mixed together in equal parts to comprise the wetting agent. The alcohol better enables the paper to absorb the water. Isopropyl rubbing alcohol has a strong odor, but the fumes are safe for human inhalation. Ethanol grain alcohol has mild fumes that are relatively safe for human inhalation. Either one may be used in the lab.

Miscellaneous Supplies

- *Clean rags*
- *Glass jars* for soaking brushes and for storing adhesives
- *Binder's thread* (linen, acid-free)
- *Sewing tape (or binding tape)*—these are the supports one sews onto during the hand-sewing process (100 percent cotton or linen/flax, acid-free)
- *Book cloth scraps* to be used for lining
- *Apron* to protect clothing from adhesives
- *Archival repair tape (or archival document tape)*
- *De-acidification sprays and solutions* such as Bookkeeper and/or Wei T'o
- *Waxed paper*
- *Beeswax* used for waxing binder's thread to prevent tangling and knotting during sewing
- *Scrap paper* of all sizes

Part Two: The Process
Recasing a 20th- or 21st-Century Book

Before any decisions can be made regarding a book in disrepair, those making the decisions need to be aware of their options. There are many possible outcomes, and all of them (including disposal of the item) are viable, depending upon individual circumstances.

Options include:

- Dispose of the item
- Dispose of the item and acquire a replacement copy
- Leave the item "as is" and continue use until disrepair forces disposal
- Get by with a quick "patch job"
- Rebind the item in-house
- Send the item out for repair or rebinding
- Send the item to a conservator for restoration and/or conservation

Considerations include:

In general:

- Policies and mission statement of the organization
- Budget(s) and funding sources of the organization
- Interests/preferences/subject expertise of individuals and groups involved in the decision (e.g., administration, board of trustees, librarians, donors)

For the individual item:

- The item's value for historical reasons (e.g., first edition, signed copy, significant provenance)
- The item's replacement value if it is rare or out of print (Is it more expensive to replace than to repair? What staff time would be involved in replacement efforts?)
- The value of the information contained in the item (If the book is soon to be outdated, it may not be worth replacement or repair.)
- Does the organization have other copies in good condition?

The bottom line is this: Is the book worth the cost in supplies and staff time? (One hour is a reasonable amount of time to expect for the recasing of a book.)

5. Parts of a Book and Types of Damage

Parts of a Book

A typical, modern, casebound book is made up of two main parts: the *text block* and the *case*.

Text block
The text block consists of the pages that have been gathered together into *signatures*, which have in turn been fastened together by sewing or glue. An *endpaper* (or endsheet), which is a folded sheet of paper, is glued to the *shoulder* of the first page and another is glued to the shoulder of the last page. The *spine* is lined with a *hinge cloth* (or super) that is also affixed to the endpapers. If a *headband* is used, this will be applied to the top and the bottom of the text block. The *lining paper* (or spine lining) is applied last and it covers both the hinge cloth and the headband ends.

Case
The case is the outer cover (the "exoskeleton") of the text block. The purpose of the case is to protect the text block. The case consists of two pieces of *binder's board*, a *case lining* (or spine lining/inlay), and a sheet of *book cloth*.

The text block is attached to the case by gluing the endpapers and the hinge cloth to the binder's boards. The case lining is not glued to the lining paper on the text block in order that the *hollow* may form. The hollow allows for a flexible binding that will open easily. The *joint* is on the outside of the case. A properly formed joint will endure a great deal of strain yet, due to heavy use, it is usually the first area of a book to show wear.

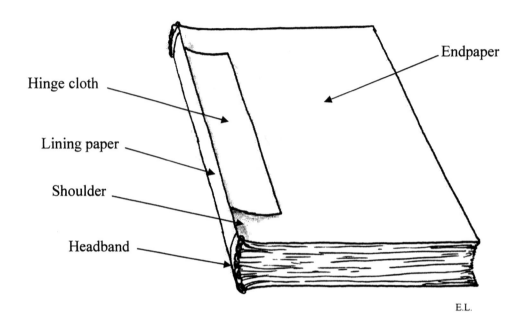

Hinge cloth

Lining paper

Shoulder

Headband

Endpaper

E.L.

The text block

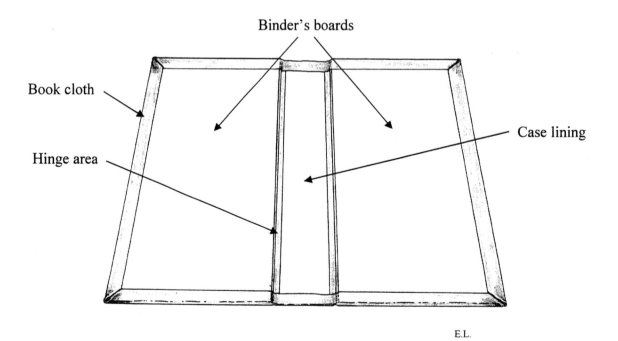

Binder's boards

Book cloth

Hinge area

Case lining

E.L.

The case

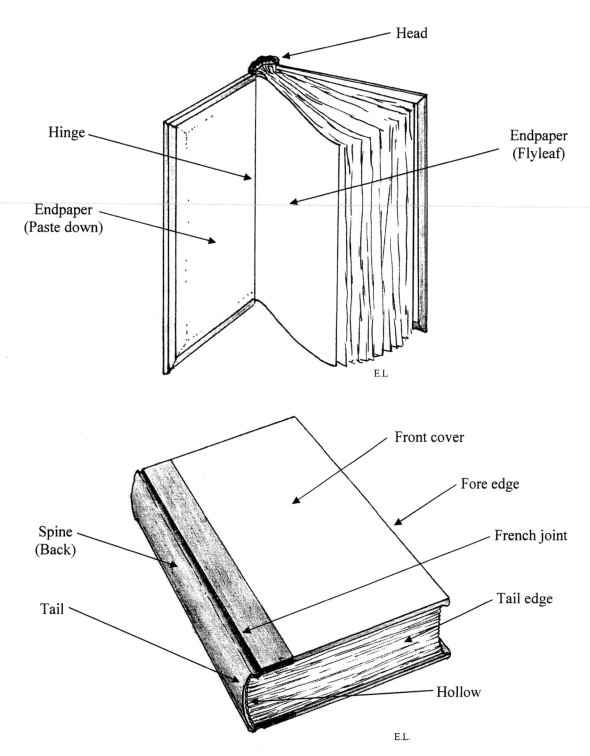

The combined case and text block

Types of Damage

Book repair corrects damage that has occurred due to abuse or repeated normal use and aging. It may also be necessary due to poorly executed original construction/manufacture. The three parts of a book that sustain damage most frequently are: the text block, the case, and the areas where the text block and the case attach.

Though most people tend to use the terms *leaf* and *page* interchangeably, they are not technically the same. The leaf is the unit that results from the folding of a sheet of paper into a signature. Each leaf consists of two pages. There is one page on each side of a leaf.

Damage to the text block
Pages from the text block may be torn, sullied, detached, or missing altogether. An entire signature may be loose or completely detached. The flyleaf half of an endpaper may become torn or detached.

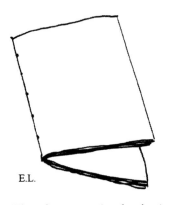

The signature (gathering)

The *signature* (or gathering) is a pamphlet, often consisting of 16 pages, that is gathered together with other signatures to form the text block. The signature is not to be confused with the *printer's signature*, which is a mark (usually a number) on the lower right corner of the first page of each signature. This mark indicates the order in which the signatures are to be sewn. The printer's signature was commonly used prior to 1920. The fold that occurs at the center of the signature is referred to as the centerfold.

Detached signature

E.L.

Detached endpaper (Flyleaf)

Damage to the case and damage to areas of text block and case attachment
The case may become sullied, worn, warped, loose, or detached. A front or back cover may become loose or detached. The head of the case may become loose. The spine of the case may become loose or detached. Hinges may become loose or broken. The paste down half of the endpapers may become torn or detached.

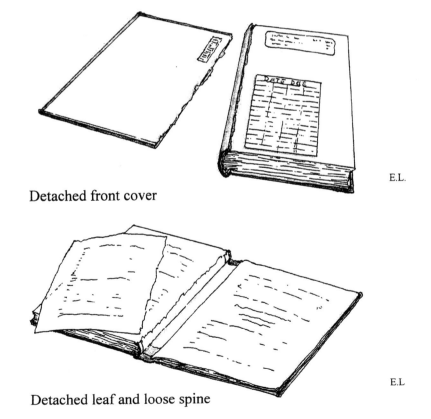

E.L.

Detached front cover

E.L

Detached leaf and loose spine

Detached case   E.L.

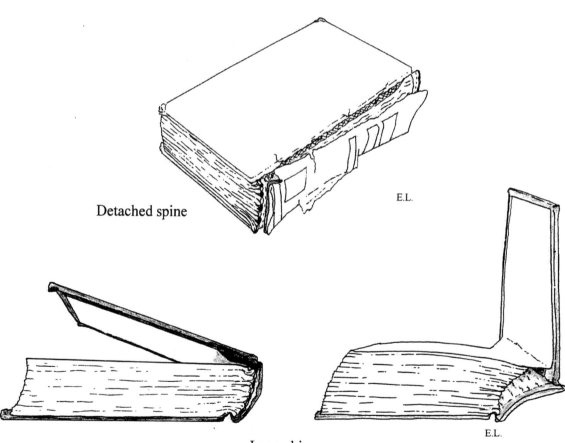

Detached spine   E.L.

Loose hinges   E.L.

6. Preservation Awareness

The following questions must be asked when selecting any materials or supplies to be used in bookbinding and/or repair procedures:

- Is it acid free or alkaline?
- Is it easily reversible?
- Is it harmless to the book/document?

Many of the suppliers and manufacturers of the supplies discussed here will provide a free "tips for use" pamphlet upon request.

Repairing Tears

When repairing a tear, first examine the tear to be certain the two sides of the tear are overlapping in the correct position. Any tear will have two frayed edges. By taking a moment to examine the edges, it will be clear that there is a correct and an incorrect position in which they must lay. If the two flaps overlap in the incorrect position, the mended page will not lie flat.

If a tear changes direction on the page, mend one direction with one piece of tape before proceeding to the next direction with a separate piece of tape.

Adhesive tape

There are two schools of thought when it comes to commonly available commercial tapes (such as Scotch™ tape). Many items in a collection are expected to have a relatively short circulation period before removal from the collection and disposal. (Various paperbacks and magazines fit into this category.) Some find it wasteful to use the more expensive archival repair tape on these items. On the other hand, some feel that not all lab staff have enough collection management experience to make distinctions regarding the most appropriate tape choices and find it impractical to set items aside until an experienced staff member can make a determination and sort the items into categories, again setting the items aside until lab staff can make the repairs. In this case, a decision may be made to use archival repair tape at all times.

Archival repair tape

When a decision is made to use tape for minor repairs on documents and books expected to remain in the collection for any length of time, archival repair tape should be used. This type of tape is generally more expensive than are more commonly known commercial brands, but it is non-yellowing as well as thinner and less rigid. Tape that is thinner and less rigid decreases chances of more damage around the repaired area with time and wear. In some situations, some archival tapes may not adhere well. If this is the case, repair the page with the tape, cover the repair with thin blotter paper, and then use a warm iron to "set" the tape.

Japanese paper and starch paste

Tears repaired with archival repair tape are typically not as strong and do not last as well as those repaired with Japanese paper (sometimes referred to as *kozo* or *Oriental paper*) and starch paste. The Japanese paper and starch paste process is used for items of high value to the collection, as it is a time-consuming process.

The ink on the item must be stable. Test this by wetting a cotton swab and lightly brushing it onto a very small area of print. After it soaks in, blot the wetted area. If the ink fades or runs, the ink is not stable. Use archival repair tape to mend the item. If the ink is stable, prop the item into a secure position so that it may be worked upon without fear of movement. Bricks covered with a soft material are often employed for this purpose.

Waxed paper must be used so that the starch paste does not seep through from one page to the next. Place one sheet of waxed paper between the page to be mended and the page that follows. Tear a strip of the Japanese paper to a size slightly longer than the tear and about 1/2″ wide. For the length of the repair strip, tear with the grain of the Japanese paper. Place the strip on a clean surface and brush the paste on the length of it, with the grain. Use tweezers to place the Japanese paper strip onto the tear. If necessary work the strip into the desired position with the tweezers. A spatula may also prove useful. Place a second piece of waxed paper over the area and place a press board and weight on top of that. Allow the item to dry for at least one hour.

Most tears extend to the edge of the page. In this case, allow the Japanese paper strip to extend over the edge of the page. Once the initial step of the repair has dried, trim the Japanese paper to approximately 1/8″ past the page edge, apply starch paste, and fold it over to the other side of the page. Repeat the rest of the process as described above.

Grain Short/Grain Long

Grain long is a term used in the manufacture of paper to indicate that the grain of the paper is running parallel to its length. *Grain short* indicates that the grain of the paper is running perpendicular to its length. Paper is made of fibers, each of which has a length. When paper is made, most of the fibers will align in the same direction. The grain is the direction in which most of the fibers lie vertically in a book cloth or paper. The grain direction should be indicated on the manufacturer label. Check the length and width measurements. Often the grain direction is indicated by the underlining of one of the measurements or the order of the measurements. However, once paper or cloth have been cut into smaller sizes, it may become difficult to remember how the material first arrived from the manufacturer. Paper and book cloth are usually rolled grain long. To assist in the grain determination, it is helpful to keep in mind that a strip of material will usually curl in the direction of grain long.

When working with paper and cloth, always make sure that the grain direction is grain long. In other words, the grain should run parallel with the spine. This assures the staff is working *with* the material, as opposed to fighting against it. Working grain long decreases the chance of wrinkles and poor creases, assuring that the pages will turn more easily and that the cover will open and close more easily. This may in turn increase the lifespan of the repair. In addition, if the grain of the paper does not run parallel to the spine, the loose ends of the paper may swell and shrink with humidity changes. This may cause buckling and may weaken the binding, eventually breaking it.

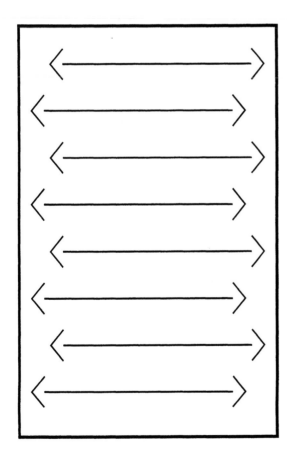   

R.D.W.

Grain short   Grain long

De-acidification Sprays and Solutions

Books, documents, and other items often contain acid. The more acid an item contains the more the item will degrade chemically, resulting in a decrease in lifespan. Paper is made from organic material (cellulose fibers). Paper products made of wood pulp (which became common during the 1800s) often contain a great deal of acid, though some modern processes have greatly reduced the problem. De-acidification neutralizes acids and increases the lifespan of the treated items.

De-acidification can be accomplished through various mass de-acidification processes by shipping collections to a facility equipped for the procedure. De-acidification can also be conducted in-house with dips or sprays, such as Bookkeeper and Wei T'o. These products come in aerosol and non-aerosol forms.

Bookkeeper

Preservation Technologies, L.P.
111 Thomson Park Drive
Cranberry Township, PA 16066

Toll Free: (800) 416-2665
Local: (724) 779-2111
Fax: (724) 779-9808

Email: info@ptlp.com

http://www.ptlp.com

Wei T'o Associates, Inc.
21750 Main Street, Unit #27
Matteson, IL 60443-3702

Local: (708) 747-6660
Fax: (708) 747-6639

Email: weito@weito.com

http://www.weito.com

Archival Storage Supplies

It makes no sense to expend resources on de-acidification if the item is then stored in an acidic environment. Also, in some cases, the best way to protect an item from further damage is proper storage. For cases such as these, lab staff should become familiar with archival paper, tissues, storage boxes, and the like. The following are reliable suppliers of conservation, restoration, and preservation supplies, including storage materials.

Gaylord Bros.
P.O. Box 4901
Syracuse, NY 13221-4901

Toll Free: (800) 448-6160
Fax: (800) 272- 3412

Email: customerservice@gaylord.com

http://www.gaylord.com

Light Impressions
P.O. Box 787
Brea, CA 92822-0787

Toll Free: (800) 828-6216

http://www.lightimpressionsdirect.com

University Products, Inc.
517 Main Street P.O. Box 101
Holyoke, MA 01041-0101

Toll Free: (800) 336-4847
Fax: (800) 532-9281

Email: custserv@universityproducts.com

http://www.universityproducts.com

Encapsulation

Encapsulation is the process of sealing valuable or fragile documents between sheets of neutral polyester so that such documents may receive extra support and be protected in microenvironments. Polyester film (such as Mylar^{TM} or Melinex^{TM}) protectors may be purchased, or the documents may be custom encapsulated. In either case, it is important to remember that the documents should never be completely sealed. In airtight environments, temperature changes are likely to cause condensation, which could create conditions sufficient for the growth of molds.

Documents should be de-acidified prior to being encapsulated. Some items, such as some art (charcoal drawings for example) should not be encapsulated. The medium may rub off onto the polyester film.

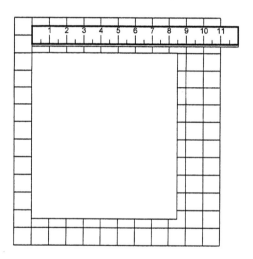

The encapsulation process is quite simple. Measure the document to be encapsulated and select or cut two pieces of polyester so that the polyester is larger than the document. Place the first sheet of polyester on a grid.

Place the document on the first sheet of polyester. Use the grid for alignment.

Measure four pieces of archival double-sided tape. Peel one side and press the exposed adhesive side to the polyester sheet. Remember to leave a small space at one corner. Be careful not to let the adhesive touch the document. Peel and expose the other side of the tape.

Very carefully place the second sheet of polyester onto the now exposed adhesive. Many find it useful to work from one corner, across the document diagonally. Some prefer to work with a partner during this phase of the process.

RDW

The document may now be handled and viewed with greater safety.

Unlike lamination, which binds the document to the plastic, the encapsulation process is easily reversible. The polyester capsule need only be cut with a scissors and the document removed.

7. Preparing the Text Block

The first question to ask when considering the recasing of a book is: Is the case protecting the text block? If the answer to that question is "yes," staff may decide to leave the book "as is," despite appearances. If the answer to that question is "no," and the text block is worth the effort, the recasing process begins.

If the choice of recasing has been selected, the following items are needed:

Equipment:
- Laying press (see page 10)
- Press boards (see pages 9, 18)

Tools:
- Straight edge (see page 15)
- Self-healing mat (see page 15)
- Scissors (see page 16)
- X-Acto™ knives (see pages 16-17)
- Bone folder (see page 17)
- Spatula (see pages 17-18)
- Glue brush (see page 19)
- Rounding hammer (see page 21)
- Backing hammer (see page 21)

Supplies:
Again, be sure to select materials that conform to current preservation standards.
- PVA (see pages 23-24)
- Starch paste (see page 24)
- Cellulose gum (see page 25)

- Hinge cloth (see page 26)
- Headband cloth (see page 26)
- Endpapers (see page 28)
- Lining paper (see page 28)
- Waxed paper (see page 29)
- De-acidification spray (see pages 29, 42)

In some cases, a portion of the original cover may be saved (see Chapter 13, "Saving Provenance"). Such a decision will depend upon the need or desire to preserve the original appearance. This may maintain the value or history of the book. In the vast majority of cases, this effort is not worth the expense of staff time.

Remove the Existing Case

Preparing the text block for recasing entails getting rid of everything associated with the old case and "cleaning up" the remaining text block. This includes the endsheets. (Many feel that endsheets are part of the case, *not* the text block—partly because they are applied by the binder, *not* the printer.) In some cases, the endsheets and/or case may be salvaged for reuse.

Begin by cutting the old book case off at the hinges. Cut through the various hinge layers with a sharp knife. There are three distinct layers at the hinge:

- Covering material (usually book cloth)
- Endsheets
- Hinge cloth

Remove the Spine Linings

1. Place the text block securely in a laying press and remove all spine linings, hinge cloth, and paper. The purpose of these linings is to stiffen the spine. The "teamwork" holds it all together and gives the spine structure. The goal at this point is to expose the bound text block.

2. The first visible layer is a lining paper. Simply scrape it away with a dull knife and spatula.

3. The next layer is the hinge cloth. Once this is also scraped away, some dried adhesive will remain. Scrape as much of this away as can be easily removed.

4. Use a de-acidification spray to neutralize existing acids and to buffer against re-acidification.

5. Brush on the cellulose gum solution to dissolve old glue and other debris. Cover this with wax paper (or Mylar™) to prevent evaporation. When sufficient absorption has occurred, scrape away the debris. Take care not to cut the binding thread or scrape away the knots. Repeat the process if necessary, but keep in mind there is no need for perfection. If stubborn

areas persist, they are not worth the effort of removal. The goal is to provide enough clean surface area so that the new lining will have sufficient area on which to adhere.

6.   Allow time for the spine to dry and harden before proceeding.

7.   The text block may then be removed from the press.

Please note: Once the hinge cloth has been cut away, staff may find that the book has been bound with a plastic adhesive. Plastic adhesive may be detected by its waxy feel. Another indication will be a text block consisting of single sheets of paper, rather than paper that has been folded and gathered into signatures. If this is the case, a knife should be used to score the spine with a crosshatch pattern. The purpose is to create a surface to which the PVA can adhere. Scoring increases surface area, generating a greater surface to which the adhesive may adhere.

E.L.

Score the spine of a book that has been bound with plastic adhesive

At this point the text block must be examined to determine if it is solid. If the text block is solid, proceed to the next section of this chapter, "Give Shape to the Text Block." If the text block is not solid, it will have to be resewn. Proceed to Chapter 8, "Resewing," and then return to the next section of this chapter.

Give Shape to the Text Block

Examine the text block to determine if it has kept its shape. If not, the proper shape must be returned to the text block. If this process is necessary, the following items will be needed:

- Laying press/finishing press (see page 10)
- Press boards (see pages 9, 18)
- Rounding hammer (see page 21)
- Backing hammer (see page 21)

Rounding
The sewing thread adds a thickness to one side of the text block that does not exist at the other. Rounding the text block distributes the thickness of the sewing threads in such a way as to make the width at the shoulder of the text block and the width at the fore edge of the text block the same.

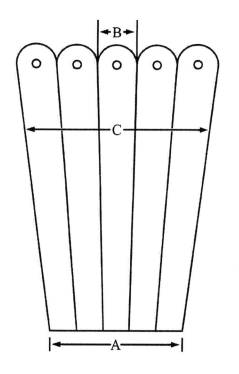

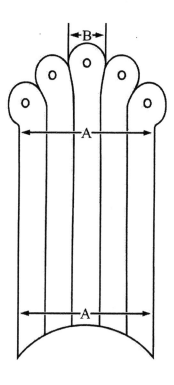

R.D.W.

Before rounding   After rounding

Before rounding, the text block is of different widths at the spine and the fore edge (widths "A" and "C"). After rounding, the text block is of the same width at the spine and the fore edge (widths "A"). The widths of the signatures at the spine remain the same (width "B").

Press the fore edge with the thumb while pounding the spine with a rounding hammer. Work your thumb and the hammer in such a way as to create a concave shape in the fore edge and a convex shape at the spine.

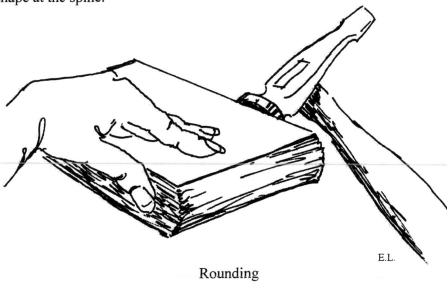

E.L.

Rounding

Backing

In essence, backing smashes the gatherings in order to form an angle. The process of backing creates the shoulders or "bumpers." This gives the text block a place for the binder's board to butt up against, which in turn helps to create the French joint and hinge. Place the text block tightly in the finishing press and use the hammer to pound the edges of the spine. The goal is to form a nearly 90-degree angle at the crease. The use of press boards will assist with this process. (Backing must be done by hand, whereas rounding will often occur as a result of pressure applied by the press.)

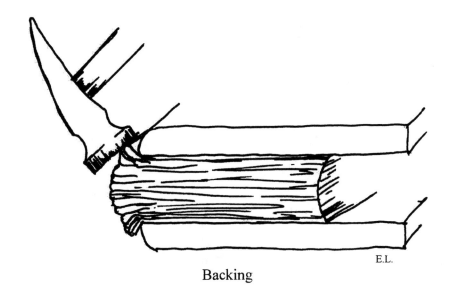

E.L.

Backing

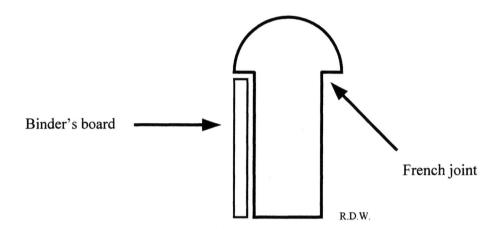

Binder's board $\longrightarrow$

French joint

R.D.W.

Backing gives the text block a place for the binder's board to butt
up against, which in turn helps to create the French joint and hinge.

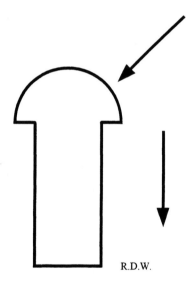

R.D.W.

Using the hammer, strike the back of the text block one-third of
the way up. Use a downward, pulling motion during the strike.

Gluing Up

Once the text block has been formed correctly, *set* it (freeze the text block into place) by applying
an adhesive (PVA) layer to the spine and place it into a press. The goal here is to freeze the threads,
knots, and book shape in place and to ensure that all of the individual gatherings become one unit.
This is called *gluing up* (also called *anchoring*).

Apply the Linings and Headbands

The following items will be needed:

- Scissors (see page 16)
- Glue brush (see page 19)
- PVA (see pages 23-24)
- Starch paste (see page 24)
  Rice starch paste works well for this process, using 6 parts water to 1 part powdered starch.
- Hinge cloth (see page 26)
- Headband cloth (see page 26)
- Lining paper (see page 28)

The Procedure:
The text block should still be in a press at this point. Remember to work grain long with paper and cloth (see pages 40-41).

Hinge cloth
Cut a piece of hinge cloth. The length should come within 1/2" of both the top and the bottom of the spine. The width must be at least 1/2" wider than the spine on both sides. It is not critical that the hinge cloth be cut straight. It will not show. Press the hinge cloth onto the wet PVA. Mold it around the spine edges. The starch in the hinge cloth will begin to soften and become malleable. The hinge cloth must adhere securely to the text block. Allow between 1 and 1-1/2 hours to dry.

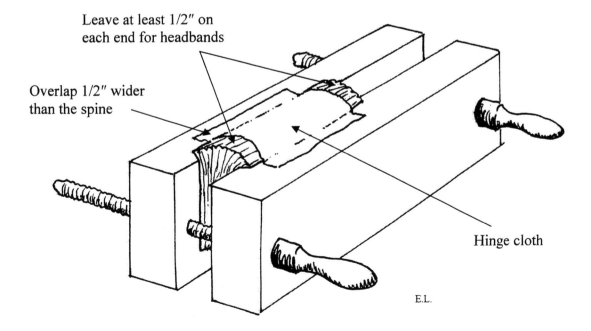

Leave at least 1/2" on each end for headbands

Overlap 1/2" wider than the spine

Hinge cloth

E.L.

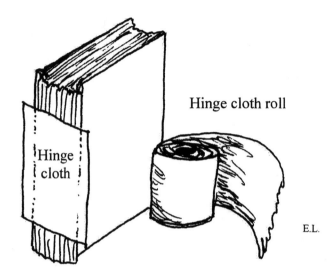

Hinge cloth roll

Hinge
cloth

E.L.

Headbands

Headbands are applied at the top and bottom of the spine of the book. In times past, the headband at the head of the book was referred to as the *headband* and that at the tail, the *tailband*.
Today both are referred to as headbands. Also in times past, they were an integral part of the
book. They were used in lieu of kettle stitches as they were integrated with signatures in the
sewing of the text block. As part of a book's construction, they provided additional support as
the reader pulled the book from a shelf. Today they are there for decorative purposes only.

To attach the headbands, make a shoulder-to-shoulder measurement by using a piece of scrap
paper and placing it against the spine. Mark each shoulder edge on the paper. Use this measure
to cut the two headbands.

E.L.

Making the shoulder-to-shoulder measurement for headband application.

Apply adhesive to the "pretty" side of the headbands (this will be obvious) and adhere them to the spine. Apply them so that the colored part shows—so they stick out slightly, above and below the text block.

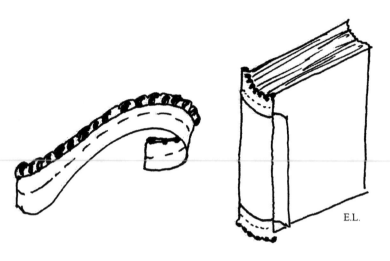

Headband cloth and text block with applied headbands.

Lining paper
The last layer to be applied to the spine is the lining paper. This material needs to be alkaline, strong, and flexible. The thinner the lining paper, the flatter the book will lie. Handmade paper is ideal for this purpose and a good choice is a *Japanese paper* (sometimes referred to as *kozo* or *Oriental paper*). This is not rice paper. It is kozo paper made from mulberry plants found in the highlands of Japan. Keep in mind that handmade paper may have no sizing and might have a tendency to swell.

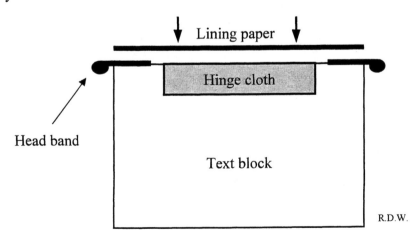

The lining paper covers both the hinge cloth and most of the headband cloth.

Measure the length of the lining paper from headband to headband, leaving the colored portion of the headband exposed. No ruler is necessary. Just place, fold, and cut. Better yet, tear the lining paper using a straight edge. The resulting feathered effect will be less noticeable. Use the shoulder-to-shoulder measurement for the width. Apply adhesive to the lining paper and press it onto the spine. The colored areas of the headbands should still be exposed. Three hours is a reasonable drying time.

The spine lining stiffens the spine of the book. This is necessary because if the spine is not stiff enough it may crack. When the spine lining is "doing its job" the spine of the book will curve gently when the book is opened.

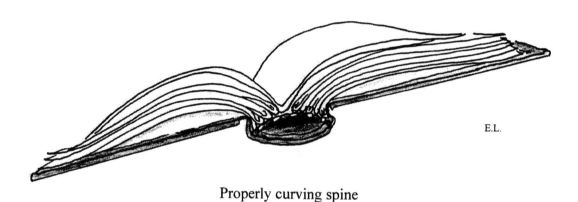

E.L.

Properly curving spine

E.L.

Cracked spine

Apply Endpapers and Any Detached Pages

The following items will be needed:

- Straight edge (see page 15)
- Self-healing mat (see page 15)
- X-Acto™ knife (see pages 16-17)
- Bone folder (see page 17)
- PVA (see pages 23-24)
- Endsheet paper (see page 28)

The Procedure:
Tipping on is the process of gluing a page down along an edge. In a perfect world, this would be cheating. In reality, it is wonderful. Although purists would sew the endpapers into the text block, most books made since the late 1800s have had their endpapers tipped on.

The signatures (gatherings) have been bent during the backing process, so the endpapers must be bent too. In other words, the endpapers must conform to the first and last signatures.

1. Fold the endsheet paper in half (grain long).

2. Use a bone folder and straight edge to make a crease.

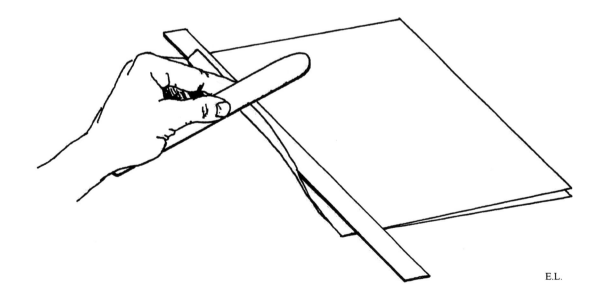

E.L.

Bend the folded edge upward.

3. Apply a bead of adhesive to the back of the bent up edge of the folded endpaper and spread it into a thin layer.

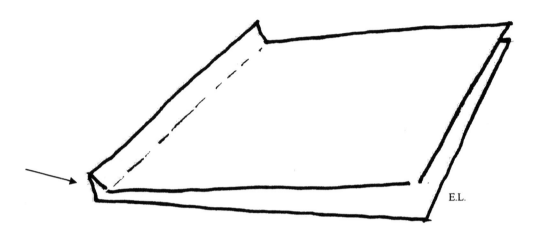

Apply adhesive to the back of the crease.

4. Place the endsheet under the shoulder, pressing with the bone folder. Do this carefully. If the endsheets are not glued down properly, the book likely will not open at page 1. It will usually open at about page 15.

The creased endsheet fits snuggly under the shoulder.

5. Trim the endsheet using a straight edge, an X-Acto™ knife, and a self-healing mat. Place the straight edge between the text block and the endsheet, lining up the straight edge with the edge of the text block. Cut the endsheet along the straight edge.

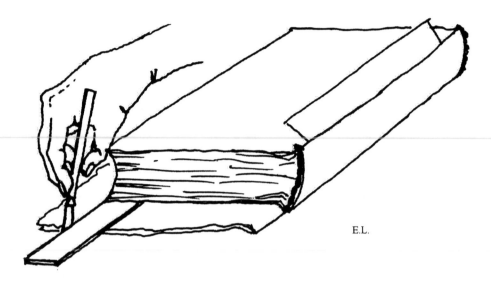

E.L.

Trim the endsheet.

6. Repeat the process on the other side of the text block.

At this point, proceed to Chapter 9, "Making the Case."

8. Resewing

The question to ask when first examining a text block is: Is the text block solid? If the answer is "yes," return to Chapter 7, "Preparing the Text Block." If the answer is "no," then chose from the following options:

- Discard the book
- Discard the book and acquire a replacement copy
- Job the book out for repair
- Resew the book in-house, by hand

If the choice of resewing has been selected, the following items are needed:

Equipment:
- Sewing frame (see page 7)
- Laying press (see page 10)

Tools:
- Self-healing mat (see page 15)
- Scissors, small (see page 16)
- X-Acto™ knife (see pages 16-17)
- Glue brush (see page 19)
- Keys (see page 20)
- Needles (see page 20)
- Awls (see page 20)

Supplies:
- Adhesive (see pages 23-25)
- Binder's thread (see page 29)

- Sewing tapes or binding tapes (see page 29)
- Apron (see page 29)
- Beeswax (see page 29)
- Archival repair tape (see pages 29, 40)
- De-acidification spray (see pages 29, 42)

There are a number of sewing techniques that may be executed by hand. The type discussed here is referred to as *tape sewing*. Sewing a text block by hand involves joining separate sections of the book (signatures or gatherings) together with thread. There are two basic methods of sewing a book: one involves sewing through the folds of the leaves and the other involves sewing through the sides of the leaves (near to the folds). The type discussed here entails sewing through the folds. Other similar forms of hand-sewing make use of chords rather than tapes. Not all books will have been sewn during their initial construction. Primarily starting in the 1960s, many books were adhesive-bound.

Procedure for Tape Sewing:

1. Take the book apart. Cut the old sewing threads and remove them.

2. If the holes remaining in the gatherings once the thread is removed are too worn to be of use, use an awl to punch fresh holes near the worn ones. Be sure the holes are made in the fold.

3. Prepare the binder's thread by *relaxing* it—pulling it repeatedly through the thumb and index finger. If the thread has not been relaxed it will twist and knot during sewing.

4. Thread the needle, leaving one end of the thread without a knot. This end may be left hanging out and tied in a square knot with thread as it emerges from the second gathering. The other end may be knotted to keep the thread from slipping through the needle.

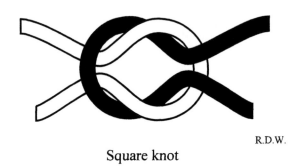

R.D.W.

Square knot

5. Apply beeswax to the thread if desired. Press the thread to the wax with the fingers of one hand and draw the thread between the wax and fingers with the other hand.

6. If new endpapers are needed (see pages 27-28), they may be treated as a gathering and sewn into the text block (rather than tipping them on by adhering them with glue, page 57).

7. If any of the folds in the gatherings are torn, reinforce them with archival repair tape. Use tape on both the inside and the outside of the fold.

E.L.

Torn folds, to be repaired prior to sewing

8. Use sewing keys to secure the sewing tapes to the sewing frame. (This process is sometimes referred to as *stringing up* and a sewing frame is said to be "strung up" once the process is complete.) Sewing tapes are the strips of cloth to which gatherings of a text block are sewn during the hand-sewing process (usually made of 100 percent cotton or linen/flax, acid-free). The ends of the sewing tape are later attached to the binder's boards. The width of the tape selected, as well as the number of tapes used, will depend upon the size of the book. Two or three tapes are commonly used and 3/4″ is a common width.

Secure one end of each sewing tape to be used to the cross bar of the sewing frame, using either a knot or a pin. Wrap the other end of each sewing tape around an "H" sewing key and fasten the key under the bed of the sewing frame. To do this, slide the key into the slot in the bed of the sewing frame with fingers or bone folder and turn the key at right angles to the slot. Be sure the tapes are taut.

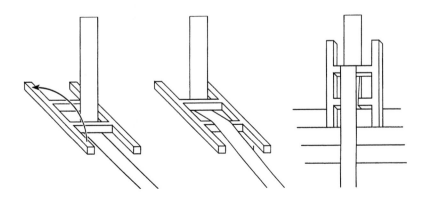

R.D.W.

Wrap the other end of the sewing tape around an "H" sewing key.
Thread as shown and flip key over. Then stand key upright.

9. Locate the first gathering and lay it on the frame. The fold will rest against the sewing tape. Work from "behind the frame." This means that the gathering folds should be closest to you.

10. Sew through the gathering from left to right and then again from right to left. Be sure to sew *around the outside* of the sewing tape. Work the needle into the prepunched holes and draw it through. Always pull the thread in the direction the needle was traveling as it exited the hole. (Pulling the thread directly toward or away from you often cuts the fold.) Do *not* pull the thread tight. There must be enough "give" so the thread will not break when the book is finished and in use. Long lengths of thread will remain inside each gathering.

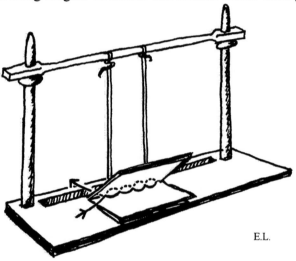

E.L.

Sewing frame showing folds resting against the sewing tapes
and direction of threads through the gathering

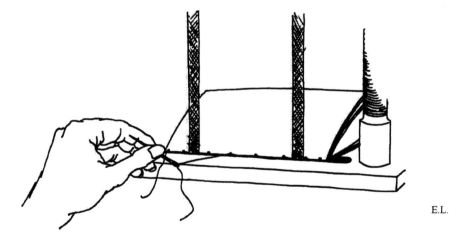

E.L.

Pull the thread in the direction the needle was traveling as it exited the hole.

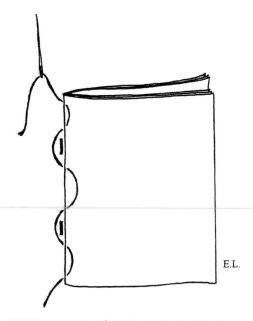

Sew around the *outside* of the sewing tape.

11. Add the next gathering and continue sewing, being sure to place a kettle knot at the end of each gathering before a new gathering is added. Always make each new knot on the *opposite* end of the previous knot.

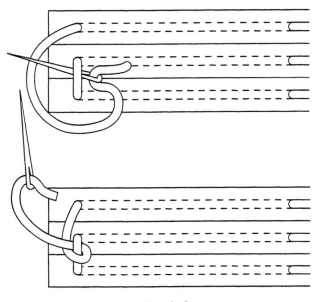

Kettle knot

12. When the thread begins to run out, leave a 4″ tail. Using a weaver's knot, knot the tail to a new thread, letting the remainder hang down. Remember to relax each new piece of thread.

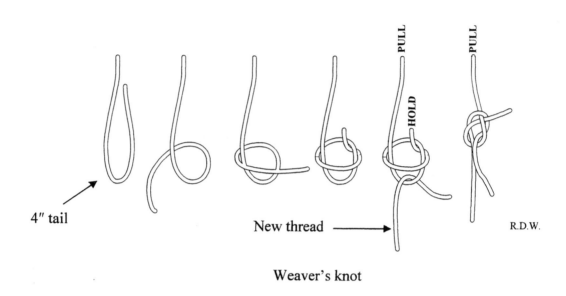

4″ tail   New thread ⟶   R.D.W.

Weaver's knot

13. When all gatherings have been sewn into place, remove the text block from the frame. Cut the tapes, leaving at least 1″ on all ends.

E.L.

Text block after sewing and removal from sewing frame

14. De-acidify the book's spine (sewing thread and tape) using a de-acidification spray.

At this point return to Chapter 7, "Preparing the Text Block" and continue with the section "Give Shape to the Text Block" (see page 50).

9. Making the Case

The *case* is the protective covering of a text block.

The following items will be needed:

- Book cloth (see pages 25-26)
    In most cases, a rather large piece is needed. A common measure is 18″ x 10 to 12″.
- Binder's board (see pages 26-27)
    Choose a thickness that is less than the depth of the shoulder of the book. The original board may be in usable condition. If so, peel off the old cloth and proceed. Most often, however, this is not worth the effort.

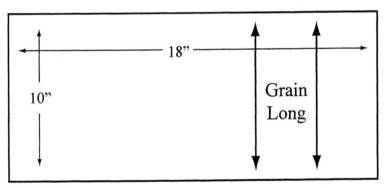

- Case lining material (see page 29)
    This material must be flexible and preferably stronger than paper. Scraps of book cloth are ideal. Never use a case lining material that is thicker than the book cloth being used for the case. If a thicker material is used, it will act as the edge of a knife against the

book cloth. Over time the spine covering will flap off. This may also occur if the case lining material is not grain long.

- Board shears (see page 11)
- Ruler (see page 15)
- Straight edge (see page 15)
- Self-healing mat (see page 15)
- Shears (see page 16)
- Bone folder (see page 17)
- PVA adhesive (see pages 23-24)
- Clean rag (see page 29)
- Scrap paper (see page 29)

The Procedure:

1. Measure and cut the binder's board. The measurements are always relative to the text block. To measure the width, place the ruler on the text block and slide it toward the shoulder until it "hits" the upturn (the rise of the shoulder). Measure from that point to the fore edge of the text block. To measure the length, use the ruler to measure from the head edge to the tail edge of the text block (from top to bottom) and add 1/4″. Use a board shears or guillotine to cut the binder's board.

E.L.

Measure the text block for the dimensions of the binder's boards.
Width: The rise of the shoulder to the fore edge of the text block
Length: Length of text block plus 1/4″

2. Place the cloth "right side" down on the self-healing mat. The right side is the coated or painted side. It is usually shiny.

3. Apply adhesive sparingly to one side each of the binder's boards. Using a glue brush, "paint" from the middle of the board outward in a spoke-like fashion. This method helps to prevent the adhesive from slopping over the edges of the board.

4. Place one of the boards down on the left side and the "wrong side" of the cloth (the back of the cloth) with at least 3/4″ remaining around the left and bottom edges (usually no more than 1″). Take hold of the cloth and board together and turn them over. Press down on the right side of the book cloth to adhere it to the binder's board, also rubbing out any air bubbles. A rag may prove useful at this point.

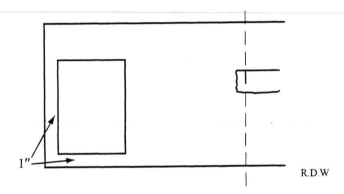

5. Using a piece of scrap paper, create a shoulder-to-shoulder measure. Using that measure, cut a strip of case lining material. The strip will be as wide as the shoulder-to-shoulder measurement and should be as long as the length of the binder's board.

   The case lining material will make up that part of the case that will end up being adjacent to the spine of the book. The case lining is sometimes referred to as the *spine lining* (or spine inlay). Most bookbinders use a piece of book cloth for this purpose. Do not use paper. Paper is not strong enough and is often too acidic.

6. There is always a gap between the case lining material and the binder's board. To create the correct amount of space, place the text block on the adhered piece of binder's board leaving at least 1/8″ of the board showing on three sides (head edge, tail edge, and fore edge). Make pencil marks where the shoulder touches the book cloth. Add 1/16″ for medium size boards and 1/8″ for heavy size boards.

7. Remove the text block. Apply adhesive on the back of the case lining and apply it to the book cloth.

E.L.

Step 6, from previous page

8. Apply adhesive to the second binder's board and secure it to the book cloth. Use a straight edge to be sure the second board is in line with the first. Also make sure there is another slight gap between the case lining and the second board. This may be done by sight. While the adhesive is still workable, nudge all components into their optimum positions. Turn the cloth and boards over once more and again work out any air bubbles.

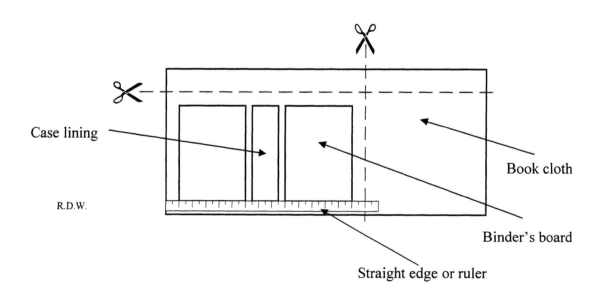

Case lining

Book cloth

Binder's board

Straight edge or ruler

R.D.W.

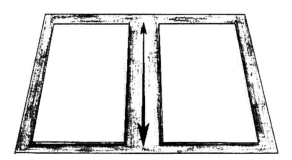

E.L. & R.D.W.

Remember to work grain long with the book cloth. Pictured above is a piece of book cloth with both binder's boards placed upon it. The arrow indicates the grain long direction.

9. Using a 1″ wide ruler or straight edge, mark a 1″ border around the boards. Two of the edges should already have been positioned 1″ from the book cloth edge, leaving only two to be cut. Cut with a straight edge and knife or with a scissors. If using a straight edge and knife, forgo the step of marking the book cloth.

Turning in:
To keep the binder's board from fraying, especially at the vulnerable corners, the book cloth will be used to cover all edges. This process is referred to as *turning in*. There are multiple methods of turning in, with most variations entailing techniques for turning in at the corners of the binder's boards. The technique outlined here is commonly used and holds up well.

10. Begin by trimming the corners at a 45-degree angle. *Do not* cut all the way to the binder's board. Leave a slight gap (about 3/16″).

    If you have not already done so, this is a good time to place a large piece of scrap paper under the book cloth to contain the glue.

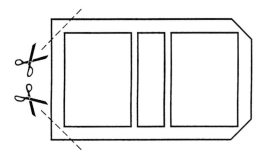

R.D.W.

Cut the corners of the book cloth at 45-degree angles.

11. Apply adhesive to the long edges, as these are the edges that will get turned over first. While the top long edge begins to set (become tacky), apply adhesive to the bottom long edge. Use a bone folder to fold the cloth of the top long edge down, adhering it to the binder's board. Use the bone folder to rub out any air bubbles. Do the same with the bottom long edge.

12. At the corners, tuck the cloth edges in with the bone folder. Do this by pressing a bit of the cloth from the top edge around the corner and then to the side of the board. It is very important that *all* of the edges be sealed, but the corners most especially. Take care to ensure cleanly folded corners. It will take some practice to learn how to best "massage" the book cloth over the corners.

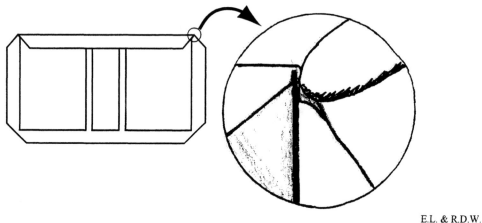

E.L. & R.D.W.

On the left: Turn in the long edges of the book cloth first.

On the right: Use a bone folder to tuck the cloth edges in over the corners.
(Enlarged view of upper right corner)

13. Apply adhesive to the short edges and turn them in, finishing the case. At this point, no binder's board edges should be exposed.

14. Check to make sure the case fits. The case will stick out slightly from the text block. This difference in size better protects the text block. It is better that the case be too big than too small.

This is the time for hot foil stamping, if desired. Follow the manufacturer's instructions for the particular hot foil stamping machine and foil used in the lab. Otherwise, proceed directly to the *casing in* process, Chapter 10, "Casing In." It is important to do so without delay, in order that the boards do not warp and the spine remains pliable enough to form a curve.

10. Casing In

Casing in is the process of attaching the case to the text block.

The following items will be needed:

- Combination laying press and press boards or platens (see pages 9-10, 18)
- Bone folder (see page 17)
- PVA adhesive (see pages 23-24)
- Blotter paper (see page 28)
- Clean rag (see page 29)
- Scrap paper (see page 29)

The Procedure:

1. If you have not already placed the text block in the case to check for fit, do so now. Then open the top cover and place a piece of scrap paper into the endsheet fold. This is done to protect the rest of the text block from dripping adhesive.

2. Apply adhesive to the paste down (the top endpaper). Start under the hinge cloth and glue that down first, using a bone folder to smooth it down.

3. Apply adhesive to the rest of the paste down (endpaper), working from the center toward the edges. Again, paint the adhesive onto the paper from the middle outward in a spoke-like manner. At this stage, throw the scrap paper away—*far away*.

The endpaper will have a tendency to curl and will need to be held down. If it curls under itself, it will stick to the next page. This could have disastrous effects.

4. Place the cover of the case onto the paste down (endpaper) and press it firmly into place. Open the cover and use a clean rag to rub out any air bubbles. The case is now in place on one side. If the positioning is not quite right, there is a window of 10 to 15 seconds to move things around before the adhesive sets.

5. Place blotter paper between the fold of the endsheet to speed the drying process and prevent sticking. Blotter paper acts as a big, thick paper towel, mopping up excess moisture. It also helps to prevent the turn-in from leaving an impression on the first sheets of paper. Blotter paper may be reused, but for the casing in process, the newer the better.

Scrap paper

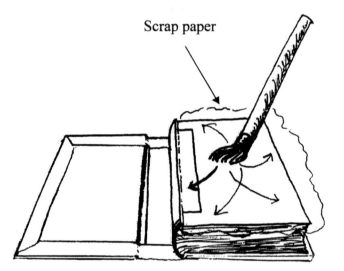

E.L.

Adhesive application during the casing in process

6. *Setting the joint*
   At this stage the joint, or hinge area, must be formed. Use a bone folder and apply firm pressure and a rubbing motion to the shoulder indent. The crease must be molded before the adhesive film sets. This is called *setting the joint* and a *French groove* or *French joint* is the result.

7. Repeat steps 1–6 for the back cover of the case.

Appearance of book after paste down (endpaper) has been adhered to the case

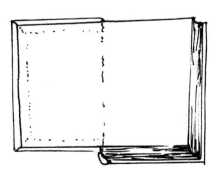

E.L.

8. *Apply nipping pressure*
    Nipping pressure must now be applied. This is an extreme pressure that forces the book into shape and that maintains the shape it has already been given. If the PVA dries without nipping pressure, the book will not hold the shape of the shoulders, grooves, and concave shape of the text block at the fore edge. Use a standing press with brass edges on the press boards. The brass edges are a must.

    Position the book so that the brass edges fit into the French grooves. Screw down the boards as tightly as possible and press the book under high pressure for 5-7 minutes.

9. After 5-7 minutes have passed, remove the book and check for any adhesive oozing. If no final alterations are needed, return the book to the standing press for at least 2 hours. A longer time period is preferable if the press time is available. After 20 hours, however, the apparatus is just being wasted.

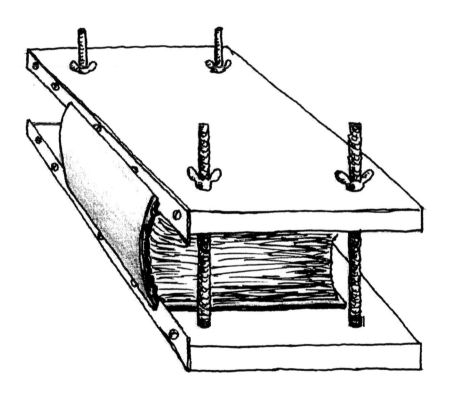

E.L.

Application of nipping pressure, using a standing press and brass-edged press boards

11. The Hollow Tube

Most books bound for library use have what is known as a *hollow back* at their spine. This is sometimes referred to as *hollow back binding* or *hollow back construction*. A hollow back binding is a binding with a space between the spine of the text block and the corresponding book cloth of the case. The book cloth of the case is attached at the joints, not at the spine, creating a hollow. The purpose of the hollow is to allow for a flexible binding that will open and close easily. This increases the durability of the book. This form of construction also decreases wear on spine lettering as there is less movement of the book cloth at the spine. Most of the movement occurs at the spine of the text block as the book is opened and closed.

In the type of in-house book binding discussed in this text, the case lining has been glued to the book cloth and the lining paper has been glued to the text block on top of the hinge cloth and head bands. Therefore, the space created is actually that between the case lining and the lining paper. Generally, this type of hollow back is considered sufficient and appropriate for in-house binding.

Sometimes a decision will be made to use a *hollow tube* in the binding process. There is some debate regarding the usefulness of the hollow tube. The proponents of the hollow tube feel it provides reinforced construction to the book. Opponents feel the hollow tube does not reinforce "text block to case" attachment and is not only unnecessary, but hinders the opening and closing of the book. Regardless of one's opinion in this debate, staff may be called upon to execute the hollow tube binding method. Therefore, a common form of this procedure will be outlined here.

Three common types of hollow tube construction are *one on, one off* (or *Oxford hollow*), *one on, two off*, and *two on, one off*. Materials appropriate for the hollow tube include paper or cloth, such as buckram or linen. The material selected should be sturdy, but flexible. For one on, one off hollow tube construction, a strip of material is measured to twice the width of the spine and is folded in half lengthwise. It is trimmed to match the length of the spine just short of the decorative strips of the headbands. One half of the resulting tube is glued to the spine of the text block while the other is glued to the corresponding section of the case. The one off, one on hollow tube is clearly not as structurally sound as the one off, two on or the two off, one on constructions.

"One on, two off" and "two on, one off" hollow tube constructions
This method will produce either the one on, two off construction or the two on, one off construction, depending on which way the hollow tube is adhered. In addition, variations may be achieved by adding additional spine width measures to the paper and increasing the number of folds (for example, *two on, two off* and so on). Proponents of this method feel it provides a reinforcing mechanism that assists in holding the text block to the case. Some feel it is particularly beneficial when working with wide or large text blocks, text blocks that are heavy in weight, books that receive particularly heavy use, or when reduced flexibility in the opening and closing of the book is desired. This causes the paper to do more of the bending, as the spine does less.

The following items will be needed:

- Combination laying press and press boards or platens (see pages 9-10, 18)
- Ruler (see page 15)
- Straight edge (see page 15)
- 25 lb. bag of lead shot (see page 16)
- Scissors (see page 16)
- X-Acto™ knife (see pages 16-17)
- Bone folder (see page 17)
- Glue brush (see page 19)
- PVA (see pages 23-24)
- Book cloth, such as starch-filled buckram or another sturdy, but flexible material (see pages 25-26). It must be able to absorb adhesive on both sides.
- Endpapers (see page 28)
- A previously existing or constructed case (see Chapter 9, "Making the Case")

The Procedure:

1. If the text block and case are still attached, remove the case and prepare the text block to receive fresh adhesive (see page 48).

2. Remembering to work grain long, trim the left edge of the selected material along the grain.

3. Use a piece of scrap paper to create a shoulder-to-shoulder measure.

4. Use the shoulder-to-shoulder measure to mark the material. Measure from the left trimmed edge and work inward, marking three times. The third measure should be decreased by 1/8″, creating a column that is 1/8″ narrower than the previous two. These marks should be created toward the top of the hollow tube material.

5. Repeat this process toward the bottom of the hollow tube material, creating three more marks.

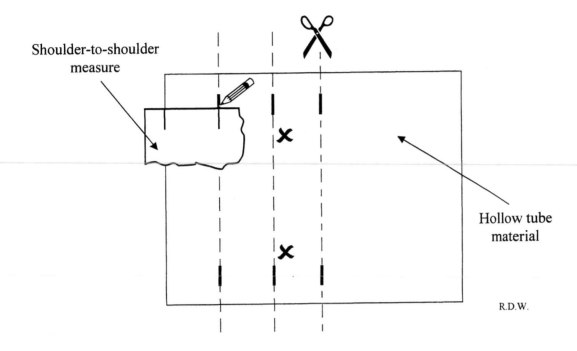

Shoulder-to-shoulder measure

Hollow tube material

R.D.W.

6. Mark the third (narrowest) strip created by this process with an "X" in several places, preferably closer to the fold line than the cut line.

7. Place the straight edge along the last pair of markings, third ones in from the edge (the two farthest right in the illustration above). Use an X-Acto™ knife to cut the material, with the grain, along the straight edge.

8. Fold the material in the same manner a letter is folded prior to being placed in an envelope. First create creases to facilitate the folding. This is done by placing the straight edge along the first pair of markings (the two farthest left in the illustration above) and by using the bone folder, or some other scoring tool, to *score* the material along this edge.

9. Repeat the scoring process along the second pair of markings (the middle two in the illustration above).

10. Flip the material over and fold it along the second scored indentation. The column with the "Xs" will be folded into place, with the "Xs" facing up.

11. Apply adhesive to the column with the "Xs" and fold along the other scored indentation so that the other outer column overlaps that of the "Xed" column. Apply pressure to ensure adequate adhesion.

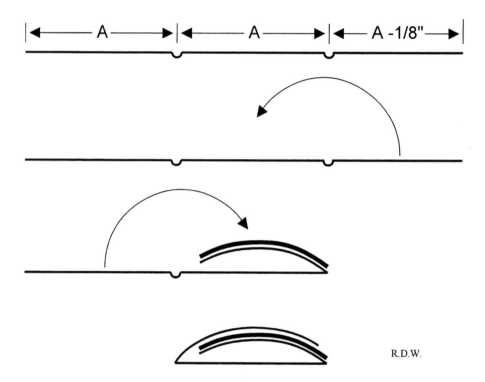

R.D.W.

At top, the hollow tube material is shown with creases separating it into three areas with widths "A", "A", and "A" minus 1/8".

The following illustrations show the smallest column being folded over onto the middle column, then the first (left) column being folded over onto the smallest. (The heavy arched line indicates the adhesive placement.)

12. The newly created tube will be doubled in thickness on one side. Trim the tube just short of the decorative strip of the headbands.

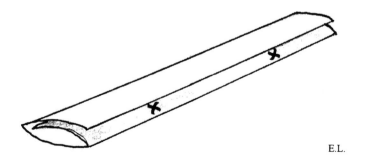

E.L.

Apply adhesive to the column with the "Xs."

13. Adhere the doubled side to the spine of the text block. This creates the two on, one off hollow tube construction. (If a one on, two off hollow tube construction is desired, simply adhere the single side of the tube to the back of the text block.)

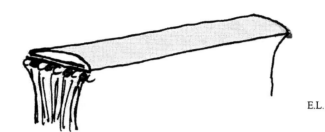

E.L.

Adhere the hollow tube to the spine of the text block.

14. If endpapers need to be applied, do so at this point (see pages 57-59).

15. Apply a layer of adhesive to the exposed side of the hollow tube and apply a layer of adhesive to the corresponding area at the back of the case. Line them up properly and adhere the two together.

16. Rub the spine with a bone folder to ensure proper adhesion and place the book between press boards and into a laying press.

E.L.

A bag of lead shot will conform its shape to that of the spine and works well as a form of pressure to assist in proper adhesion.

12. Rebacking

Rebacking is the process of replacing the material covering the spine of a book, while reusing the original front and back covers of the case. If a substantial portion of the original spine can be salvaged, it is repaired and glued over the newly constructed spine. This is done, when possible, so that the book may keep as much of its original appearance as possible—so that the spine covering continues to match the rest of the case. Some of the new spine material will be worked *under* the original covering of the binder's boards, though much of it will remain visible. For that reason, it is important to select a rebacking material that is similar to that of the original, if the original is damaged beyond repair.

This repair technique is called into service when the covers are still firmly attached to the text block and the linings are in good repair, but the spine has become loose or detached. The rebacking process outlined here leaves the original covers of the case in place while the spine area of the case is replaced, though some will make use of a rebacking process if the covers are partially or even completely detached.

The following items will be needed:

- Press boards (see pages 9, 18)
- Ruler (see page 15)
- Straight edge (see page 15)
- X-Acto™ knife (see pages 16-17)
- Bone folder (see page 17)
- Spatula (see pages 17-18)
- Glue brushes (see page 19)
- PVA (see pages 23-24)
- Book cloth (see pages 25-26)
- Scrap paper (see page 29)

- De-acidification spray (see pages 29, 42)
- Lining material (see pages 29, 67-68)

The Procedure:

1. Make incisions into the binder's boards from the outside front and back covers of the case. Cut approximately 1/8″ from the hinge. *Do not* cut into the hinge.

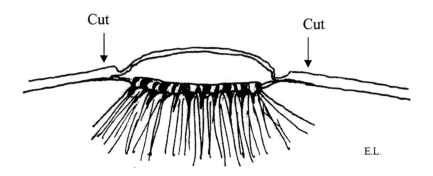

2. Peel away the spine-covering materials.

3. Using a sharp knife and spatula as needed, lift up the case-covering material from the incision to between 1/2 to 1″.

4. De-acidify the spine.

5. Use a piece of scrap paper to create a measure for the new spine-covering material. Measure from under the old case-covering material of the front cover to under the old case-covering material of the back cover. This measure need not be exact.

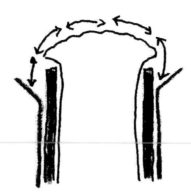

E.L.

Creating the measurement for the new spine-covering material

6. Use the newly created scrap paper measure to cut a strip of new book cloth (or whatever material has been selected for the new case-covering material). The length of the cloth should be cut to the length of the case, plus 3/4″.

7. Using another piece of scrap paper, create a shoulder-to-shoulder measure. This measure will be used to cut a new case lining. The length should measure the length of the binder's board (the height of the board if the book were standing upright, as on a shelf).

8. Apply adhesive to the back of the lining and adhere it to the new spine material.

9. Fold the spine material over the case lining.

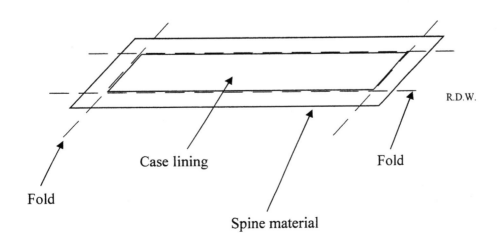

R.D.W.

Case lining

Fold

Fold

Spine material

10. Starting with the front cover, slip the new spine covering under the old case-covering material. Check for fit and correct as needed by peeling up more of the case-covering material with a knife and/or spatula.

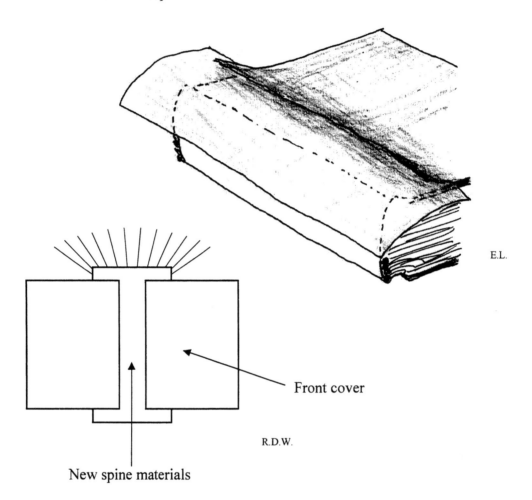

E.L.

Front cover

R.D.W.

New spine materials

11. Remove the new spine covering and apply adhesive to the binder's board where exposed (under the old case covering).

12. Reinsert the new spine covering and adhere with rubbing pressure.

13. Use a bone folder to set the French joint (see page 74).

14. Repeat steps 10 through 13 at the back cover, using both pulling and pressing to work around the spine of the text block.

15. Examine the case to determine the size of the original turn-ins and trim the new turn-ins accordingly.

16. Use a spatula if necessary to gently pry open the old turn-ins. Cut the edges of the case material if necessary.

17. Apply adhesive into the old turn-ins and also on top of the new turn-ins.

18. Tuck the new turn-in under the old turn-in and also under the original endsheets. Use your fingers to give the area a proper shape and check the shape of the French hinges once again.

19. Place the book between press boards and apply light pressure. This is to ensure that the book dries in its proper shape. Too much pressure at this point may have the opposite effect, causing the book to lose its proper shape.

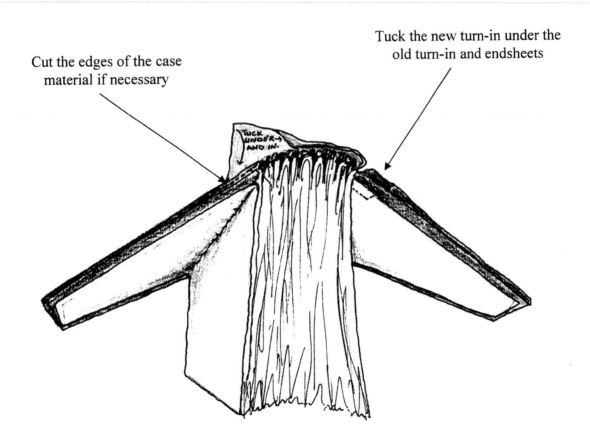

Cut the edges of the case material if necessary

Tuck the new turn-in under the old turn-in and endsheets

13. Saving Provenance

In the broad sense, provenance is evidence of a book's origin or source. By this definition, anything considered historically significant, or unique to a particular book, may be referred to as the book's provenance. This definition includes things such as the original spine or the front panel (or cover plate). Some conservators limit the definition to include only additions to a book that are not original to the book, but that provide evidence of a book's history (i.e., book plates, inscriptions, author signatures). These definitions are not to be confused with that used in the archival field. In modern archival practice, provenance (or *Respect des Fonds*) means that all documents from a single source (creator) must be kept together (must not be intermingled with other documents/records).

Rather than applying information to the spine or cover, by some method such as hot foil stamping, staff may determine that it is preferable to reuse the original spine label, front panel, or other areas of the book associated with its provenance. Saving provenance may save time in some cases; however the most common reason to save provenance is for the value it adds to the book.

The following items will be needed:

- Straight edge (see page 15)
- X-Acto™ knife (see pages 16-17)
- Spatula (see pages 17-18)
- Glue brush (see page 19)
- PVA (see pages 23-24)
- Cellulose gum (see page 25)
- Wetting agent (see page 29)

The Procedure: Spine Label

The spine-covering material will have been removed from the text block at this point and a new case will have been made.

1. Remove the old case lining from the book cloth (or other case-covering material) of the spine.

2. Use a knife to trim the spine label area intended for preservation. Remove rough edges.

3. Brush the cellulose gum solution onto the back of the spine label to remove any remaining paper fibers or other matter. Scrape away as much as possible.

4. Allow enough drying time so that the spine label becomes thoroughly dried, especially if the old adhesive had been hide glue. Wet hide glue and PVA do not adhere well.

5. Once dry, brush PVA onto the back of the spine label and apply it to the new case. Use a clean rag to rub out any air bubbles. Allow to dry.

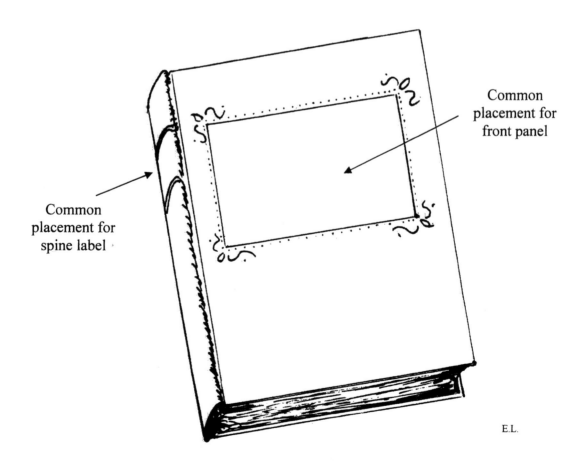

Common placement for front panel

Common placement for spine label

E.L.

The Procedure: Front Panel

A decision must be made regarding what parts of the front panel to preserve. Many front panels have border designs that create ideal cutting outlines.

1. Use an X-Acto™ knife to cut along the chosen border outline.

2. Separate the panel from the front cover by peeling it back and by splitting the binder's board. A layer of binder's board will remain adhered to the panel. This layer should be as thin as possible.

E.L.

Separate the panel from the front cover by peeling it back

3. Test the back of the panel by brushing on a small amount of cellulose gum solution to a small area. If it does not absorb immediately (turning the surface dark), spray the area with a wetting solution.

4. Brush the cellulose gum solution onto the back of the front panel to remove as much of the remaining binder's board as possible.

5. Allow enough drying time so that the front panel becomes thoroughly dried, especially if the old adhesive had been hide glue. Wet hide glue and PVA do not adhere well.

6. Once dry, brush PVA onto the back of the front panel and apply it to the front cover of the new case. Use a clean rag to rub out any air bubbles. Allow to dry.

Glossary

Acid

In chemistry, a substance capable of forming hydrogen ions when dissolved in water. Acids can weaken cellulose in fibrous plant products (such as paper) and this may lead to embrittlement. Acids may be introduced in the manufacture of books (e.g., from sizing or wood pulp) or may be introduced as the result of migration from other sources (e.g., other books, atmospheric pollution).

Acid-free

In chemistry, anything with a neutral pH of 7.0 or higher. Lower numbers are acidic. Higher numbers are alkaline.

Acid migration

The transfer of acid from one material to another of lower acidity (or pH).

Adhesive construction

A type of binding (as in many contemporary paperback books).

Adhesives

Substances that causes the adhesion of one component of a book to another.

Alkaline

Any material that has a pH greater than 7.0 may be considered alkaline.

Anchoring

The process of applying adhesive to the spine of a text block in order to freeze the threads and knots in place (also called "gluing up").

Archival, archival quality, archivally sound
Generally, terms used to describe materials that are acid free. These terms suggest that an item is enduring, durable, or chemically stable, and can therefore be safely used for conservation purposes.

BTU
A BTU (British thermal unit) is the amount of heat energy needed to raise the temperature of one pound of water by one degree Fahrenheit (also Btu or B.Th.U.).

Backing
The process that gives the text block shoulders. This creates a place for the binder's board to butt up against.

Backing hammer
The tool used to pound the shoulder into the text block.

Ballast
The ballast is an integral, energy consuming part of a fluorescent lighting fixture. It supplies the appropriate starting and running voltage and the proper current for the lamps.

Bast fibers
Fibers for Japanese papermaking from the inner bark of various shrubs. Their use makes very long-fibered, strong, but tissue-thin papers. They make a pure, natural-colored, neutral pH paper (sometimes wrongly called "rice paper").

Binder's board
The cardboard-like material that gives a hardcover book its rigidity.

Board shears
A tool that resembles a large, freestanding paper cutter with a curved blade.

Bone folder
A smooth-edged tool used as an extension of the bookbinder's fingers, for folding and burnishing.

Book cloth
Fabric that has been treated in such a way (painted or filled in) so that adhesive will not ooze through under pressure.

Book conservator
A person who works primarily on repairing, restoring, or conserving single copies of books as well as other documents.

Buckram
D and E grade book cloth.

Buffer
An alkaline reserve, which is added to an item for the purpose of counteracting acid that may migrate to the item in the future.

Buffering
The process of adding a buffer or alkaline reserve to an item. The purpose is to neutralize acidity with the addition of an alkaline substance and to provide the item with a protective reserve. Calcium carbonate is frequently used. Buffering alone does not insure that an item will remain neutral pH over time, but acts as insurance.

Caliper
Thickness of paper, binder's board, or other material.

Case
The covering (soft or hard) that protects the text block.

Case lining (or spine lining or spine inlay)
Material (usually book cloth) that makes up part of a case. After the casing in process, it will be that part of the case that lies adjacent to the spine.

Casing in
The process of attaching the case to the text block.

Cellulose
The primary component of the cell walls of plants. Also, the primary component of many fibrous plant products, including paper.

Cellulose gum
A thickening agent used to keep a surface moist or for dissolving old adhesive.

Cellulostic material
Paper, cloth, and other products made from fibrous plants.

Chemically stable, chemical stability
Terms used to describe the state of an item when it is not easily decomposed or modified chemically.

Conservation
The treatment of items that stabilizes them chemically, strengthens them physically, or in some way contributes to their longevity.

Daylight
The maximum amount of space between the platens of a press.

De-acidification
The process of chemically treating materials, that neutralizes their acidity, to prevent them from decomposing.

Double-fan gluing
The process by which a machine fans the book to be bound, then applies adhesive in such a way that each page is tipped to the next.

Drill and sew
The style (method) of binding in which the binder drills holes straight through the text block, rather than through the folds of the signatures. The block is then sewn by hand.

Durability
A determination that is gauged by the strength and lasting quality of the bond an adhesive creates, and by the length of time it takes the unused portion of adhesive to spoil.

Dutch corners
The method of folding the book cloth over the corners of the binder's board at a 45-degree angle rather than trimming it off.

Endpaper (or endsheet)
The folded sheet that is attached to both the casing and the text block. It assists in holding the two together. The half that is attached to the text block is called the *flyleaf.* The half that is attached to the casing is called the *paste down.*

Edition
The total number of books printed from one set of plates or from one setting of type, therefore being identical, and offered to the public at one time.

Encapsulation
The process of providing a protective enclosure for flat items. It involves placing the item between two sheets of transparent polyester that are then sealed around all edges leaving a slight gap for "breathing."

Ferrule
The band of metal that wraps around a round, hog's hair glue brush. It helps the brush hold its shape and bind the bristles to the head.

Fiberboard
Laminated sheets of heavily pressed fiber.

First edition
While there is some debate on the actual meaning of the term, for collecting purposes, this term is applicable only to the first printing of a book.

Flyleaf
The half of the endpaper that is attached to the text block.

Foil stamping
The process used in applying foil lettering and other insignia to new casings using a heated press.

Font
A collection of letters and sometimes other symbols, all of one design (as in a Scrabble™ set) used in printing.

French joint (or French groove/open joint)
The indentation of a book casing that is formed while "setting the joint" and by setting the board a slight distance from the shoulder. The creation of a French joint allows for a thicker cover that will still open easily.

Front panel
An area on the front cover of a book that may contain the book's title and other information. It is often decorative in nature, and may be bordered in some way. The term sometimes refers to the entire front cover of a book.

Gathering
A folded sheet or set of sheets to be sewn (or that have been sewn). A gathering constitutes a section of a text block also called a signature. The sheet is the unit referred to by the printer, the gathering is the unit referred to by the book binder.

Glue
See adhesives

Gluing up (or anchoring)
The process of applying adhesive to the spine of a text block in order to freeze the threads, knots, and text block shape in place and ensuring that all of the individual gatherings become one unit.

Grain long (*see also* grain short)
A term used in the manufacture of paper to indicate that the grain of the paper is running parallel to its length. Paper is made of fibers, each of which has a length. When paper is made, most of the fibers will align in the same direction. The grain is the direction in which most of the fibers lie vertically in a book cloth or paper. Paper and cloth are usually rolled grain long.

Grain short (*see also* grain long)
A term used in the manufacture of paper to indicate that the grain of the paper is running perpendicular to its length.

Guillotine
A cutting tool that is essential in print shops and that can be useful in bookbinding labs. The angled blade comes straight down on the materials to be cut.

Hand binder
A person who works primarily on repairing or rebinding single copies of books.

Headband
The decorative strip of cloth that is glued to the top and bottom of the spine beneath the casing.

HEPA filter (High Efficiency Particle Arrester)
The component in an air purifier that removes spores, bacteria, and other small particles from the air. The term also refers to the air purifier itself.

Hide glue
A traditional adhesive for bookbinding. It is reversible only by using heat or an enzyme-based solvent. This type of glue is no longer preferable.

Hinge
The area on the inside cover of a book (both front and back) that corresponds to the French joint on the outside of the book.

Hinge cloth
The material that, along with paper endsheets, holds the book cover onto the text block.

Hollow
The empty space at the spine of the book between the text block and the case. The purpose of the hollow is to allow for a flexible binding that will open and close easily. This increases the durability of the book. This form of construction also decreases wear on spine lettering.

Hollow tube binding
A method of repairing a binding using reinforced construction at the spine.

Hygrometer
An instrument used to measure relative humidity levels.

Hygrothermograph
An instrument used to measure and record the temperature and relative humidity, along with the date and time.

Japanese paper
Handmade paper made from the fibers of mulberry plants found in the highlands of Japan. This is not rice paper. Sometimes referred to as kozo or Oriental paper.

Job backer
A type of freestanding laying press, usually made of iron. Among other uses, it holds a book during the rounding and backing process.

Joint
See French joint

Kettle stitch
A knot tied in the thread, when handsewing, that links one thread to the next and one gathering to the next.

Keys
Tools that hold the sewing tape in place beneath the sewing frame.

Laying press
A vice-like tool that applies side-to-side pressure. It is made up of two heavy, wooden platens with two large, wooden screws. Also referred to as finishing presses.

Laying pressure
Pressure that is applied to materials in a side-to-side manner. Also known as "the pinchine effect."

Leaf
The unit that results from the folding of a sheet of paper into a signature. Each leaf consists of two pages. There is one page to each side.

Lining
The three layers of materials applied to the back of the text block: adhesive, hinge cloth, and lining paper. The term also applies to the process of creating the lining.

Lining paper (or spine lining)
A thin piece of paper that is the last layer added to finish a text block. The lining paper covers both the hinge cloth and the headbands and it stiffens the spine.

Micron
A measure of particle size. There are 25,400 microns in an inch. There are over 600 microns in the period at the end of this sentence.

Mil
A unit of thickness equaling one thousandth of an inch.

Moldmade paper (or Mouldmade paper)
A term once used to refer to paper made by hand. Now used in commercial catalogs to refer to paper made by machine (with a slowly rotating cylinder) that *approximates* the look of handmade paper.

Neutral
An item that is neither alkaline nor acid (having a pH of 7.0).

Nipping pressure
An extreme pressure that forces a book into shape (shoulders and hinges). The back of the text block becomes concave.

PVA (Polyvinyl acetate)
A colorless, transparent plastic. When used as an adhesive, it is fast-setting and fully reversible with water.

Page
One side of a leaf.

Paste down
The half of the endpaper that is attached to the casing.

Pint capacity
The number of pints of water an air conditioner can remove from the air in a 24-hour period.

Platens
The two surfaces of a press that touch the book(s) when the book(s) is pressed between them.

Point size
A unit of measure for type. There are 72 points per inch.

Preservation
The act of preventing loss, damage or change; maintaining an item in its current form to the greatest extent possible.

Press
A device used to place materials under pressure for extended periods of time, to give shape to a book or to be used as a "third hand" as a bookbinder works.

Press boards
Boards with brass edges that form a groove (French hinge) in the cover of a book.

Printer's signature (or signature mark)
The mark on the first page of each gathering used to indicate the sewing order of the gatherings. This system was used before 1920.

Provenance
In the broad sense, provenance is evidence of a book's origin or source. By this definition, anything considered historically significant, or unique to a particular book, may be referred to as the book's provenance. This definition includes things such as the original spine or the front panel (or cover plate). Some conservators limit the definition to include only additions to a book that are not original to the book, but that provide evidence of a book's history (i.e. book plates, inscriptions, author signatures). These definitions are not to be confused with that used in the archival field. In modern

archival practice, provenance (or *Respect des Fonds*) means that all documents from a single source (creator) must be kept together (must not be intermingled with other documents/records).

Rebacking
The process of replacing the material covering the spine of a book, while reusing the original front and back covers of the case.

Restoration
The act of returning something to as near original condition as possible.

Reversibility
The concept that any process executed can be undone at a future date. The ability to undo a treatment process with no change to the object.

Rounding
The process of giving the spine of a book a rounded shape. The purpose is to distribute the thickness of the sewing threads of a book. This helps to make the thickness of the book at the spine the same as that at the opposite edge.

Rounding hammer
A tool used to pound the back of the text block into a convex form.

Self-healing mat
A work mat on which cutting procedures can be performed. It protects the worktable and does not show cuts (they "heal").

Setting the joint
The process during which the binder creates the French joint or hinge.

Setting time
The length of time it takes adhesive to set. After this time period, the adhesive becomes overly tacky and unworkable.

Sewing frame
The piece of equipment used to hold sewing tape taut while sewing gatherings together.

Sewing tape
The strips of cloth to which gatherings of a text block are sewn during the hand-sewing process (usually 100 percent cotton or linen/flax, acid-free).

Shoulder
The area of the text block that lies near the spine on both the front and the back of the text block. It is the part of the text block that is bent (curved) during the backing process to form a projection outward from the text block.

Shoulder-to-shoulder measurement
Exactly as the phrase implies, this is the measurement between the shoulders of a book.

Signature
A sheet of paper that, when folded to leaf size (two pages), forms one section (gathering) of a book. This is not to be confused with the "printer's signature."

Sizing
An additive that makes paper less absorbent. It can be a glue, gelatin, cellulose, or starch. It can be added to the pulp before the sheets of paper are formed, or to the surface of the paper after the sheets are dry.

Smyth sewing
A type of machine-executed book sewing.

Spine (or back)
The folded area of a text block that exists after all signatures have been sewn. This term also refers to the same area of a text block in its case (a book). In both cases, this is the part of the text block or book that is visible as these items stand upright on a shelf.

Standing press
A press that applies top-down pressure.

Standing pressure
Pressure that is applied to materials in a top-down manner. The term also refers to a type of pressure that helps the book "memorize" its shape. This pressure is lighter than nipping pressure.

Starch-based adhesives
Plant-based adhesives, such as rice starch, that are immediately reversible with water.

Straight edge
A tool employed as a cutting guide when using utility blades.

Synthetic resin
A frequently used adhesive that is fast-setting, remains flexible and transparent when dry, and is fully reversible with water. A PVA (polyvinyl acetate) brand named Jade 403 is widely accepted in the trade because of its alkalinity.

Text block
The part of the book that remains once the cover has been removed—the pages, the gatherings (signatures).

Thermohygrometer
An instrument used to measure both temperature and relative humidity.

Thermometer
An instrument used to measure temperature.

Tipping on
The process of attaching a page (or reattaching a page that has fallen off) by brushing a thin bead of adhesive on the edge of a loose page, placing it in the angle of the shoulder, and pressing it in place using a bone folder.

Tools
For the purposes of a bindery, these are hand-held implements with a 3-5 year life span.

Turn-in
The flap of book cloth that is folded over the binder's board corners in making a new case.

Turning in
The process of folding the book cloth over the binder's board while making a new case.

UV filter
An item or material used to filter out ultraviolet (UV) rays of light.

Ultraviolet (UV) light
Light (electromagnetic radiation) with wavelengths shorter than the violet end of the spectrum of visible light. The earth's atmosphere blocks the transmission of most ultraviolet light, but enough remains (or is produced) to cause conservation concerns.

Upturn
The rise of a book's shoulder.

Wetting agent
A compound, such as alcohol, used to counter the water resistance of sizing in paper.

Manufacturers and Suppliers

The manufacturers and suppliers listed alphabetically here are those previously recommended in this text. This list is by no means exhaustive, nor is it meant to exclude others not listed here. Obtain as much information as possible from as many vendors as possible, so that comparisons of cost and product quality may be made.

Aabbitt Adhesives
2403 N. Oakley Avenue
Chicago, IL 60647
Toll Free: (800) AABBITT
Local: (773) 227-2700
Email: info@aabbitt.com
http://www.aabbitt.com/

Archivart
A Division of Heller & Usdan, Inc.
7 Caesar Place
Moonachie, NJ 07074
Toll Free: (800) 804-8428
Email: sales@archivart.com
http://www.archivart.com

Ernest Schaefer, Inc.
731 Lehigh Avenue
Union, NJ 07083-7626
Local: (908) 964-1280

Gane Brothers & Lane
Midwest Region (Corporate Offices)
1400 Greenleaf Avenue
Elk Grove Village, IL 60007
Toll Free: (800) 323-0596
Fax: (800) 784-2464
Email: sales@ganebrothers.com
http://www.ganebrothers.com/

Gaylord Bros.
P.O. Box 4901
Syracuse, NY 13221-4901
Toll Free: (800) 448-6160
Fax: (800) 272- 3412
Email: customerservice@gaylord.com
http://www.gaylord.com

General Roll Leaf Manufacturing Company
10-03 44th Avenue
Long Island City, NY 11101
Toll Free: (888) 868-1876
Local: (718) 784-3737
Email: peterb@generalrollleaf.com

ICG Holliston
P.O. Box 478
Kingsport, TN 37662
Toll Free: (800) 251-0451
http://www.icgholliston.com

The KWIKPRINT Manufacturing Company, Inc.
4868 Victor Street
Jacksonville, FL 32207
Toll Free: (800) 940-5945
Local: (904) 737-3755
Fax: (904) 730-0349
Email: kwik@fdn.com
http://www.kwik-print.com

Light Impressions
P.O. Box 787
Brea, CA 92822-0787
Toll Free: (800) 828-6216
http://www.lightimpressionsdirect.com

Preservation Technologies, L.P. (Bookkeeper)
111 Thomson Park Drive
Cranberry Township, PA 16066
Toll Free: (800) 416-2665
Local: (724) 779-2111
Fax: (724) 779-9808
Email: info@ptlp.com
http://www.ptlp.com

University Products, Inc.
517 Main Street P.O. Box 101
Holyoke, MA 01041-0101
Toll Free: (800) 336-4847
Fax: (800) 532-9281
Email: custserv@universityproducts.com
http://www.universityproducts.com

Wei T'o Associates, Inc.
21750 Main Street, Unit #27
Matteson, IL 60443-3702
Local: (708) 747-6660
Fax: (708) 747-6639
Email: weito@weito.com
http://www.weito.com

World Wide Web Resources

The World Wide Web (www or the Web) exists in a state of constant change. Web sites may be updated frequently or they may remain stagnant, in some cases becoming outdated. Some sites may disappear altogether. For these reasons, staff of a bookbinding and repair lab may wish to bookmark the following sites on their own computer(s) and edit the bookmarks as necessary. If a site is found to be extremely useful and referred to frequently, staff may find it worthwhile to save the desirable pages to their own computer or to print out the most valuable information. This is done for protection against removal of the site by its owner/host or the loss of information at the site.

A great deal of useful information (including tip sheets and guide pamphlets) may be found at the sites of various manufactures and suppliers. Some of these "how-to" guides are available for purchase and some are provided free of charge. They may either be sent by mail or may be completely online. Here are a few examples:

Brodart
http://www.shopbrodart.com/site_pages/h2guides/default.htm
"Informational and Instructional guides on buying, repairing, and using library supplies & furnishings."

A Simplified Step-by-Step Guide to Book Repair and Protection!
http://www.shopbrodart.com/site_pages/h2guides/downloadable_guides/BookRepairManual04.pdf

Carr McLean
http://www.carrmclean.ca/forms.htm
FREE Downloads

Book Repair Manual: Protecting Paperbacks—Magazines
http://www.carrmclean.ca/REPAIR_LR.pdf

One need only use search terms such as "book binding" or "book repair" with a search engine to locate many useful sites. The following list is not exhaustive. A few sites are provided here to get the reader started. Annotations are, in most cases, direct quotes from information found at the various sites.

American Institute for Conservation of Historic and Artistic Works (AIC)

http://aic.stanford.edu/

The AIC "is the national membership organization of conservation professionals dedicated to preserving the art and historic artifacts of our cultural heritage for future generations."

The Book and Paper Group Annual

http://aic.stanford.edu/sg/bpg/annual/

"The Book and Paper Group Annual is published once a year by the Book and Paper Group (BPG), a specialty group of the American Institute for Conservation of Historic and Artistic Works (AIC)."

Book Arts Web

http://www.philobiblon.com/

Book Arts Web "features links to a large selection of book arts related sites on the web, including educational opportunities, professional organizations, tutorials, reference materials, and galleries with images. This is also the home of the Book_Arts-L FAQ which features full subscription information for this listserv of almost 1500 individuals but also the full archives organized by year, then month. They are also fully searchable and contain a treasure trove of all kinds of technical tips, announcements, and helpful banter."

Book Information Website

http://www.xs4all.nl/~knops/index3.htm

Devoted to "all aspects of books, book arts, book history, letterpress printing, bookschools, book and paper restoration and conservation, paper and papermaking, book artists, bookbinding and bookbinders, antiquarian books, book search services, book auctions, individual bookdealers, manuscripts, pop-up books, history of printing."

Bookbinding: A Tutorial by Douglas W. Jones

http://www.cs.uiowa.edu/~jones/book/index.html

"Bookbinding, the art of sewing pages into a cover to make a book, can serve many purposes. This tutorial introduction is aimed primarily at those who wish to preserve the content of old pulp paperbacks by photocopying them onto archival paper and then binding the results using an archival binding technique, the long-stitch. Most of this tutorial is equally applicable to binding materials from other sources."

Bookbinding and the Conservation of Books: A Dictionary of Descriptive Terminology

Matt T. Roberts and Don Etherington, Drawings by Margaret R. Brown

http://palimpsest.stanford.edu/don/don.html

Conservation and Preservation, Washington State University; Manuscripts, Archives, and Special Collections
http://www.wsulibs.wsu.edu/holland/masc/conserve.htm

Particularly helpful is a glossary of terms and various treatment examples.

Conservation Laboratory Manual, University of Kentucky Libraries
http://www.uky.edu/Libraries/conserman.html

futureofthebook.com
http://www.futureofthebook.com/
"This web site visualizes the future of the codex book. Commentary considers hybrid topics between reading behaviors, traditional book use in the context of digital delivery systems, library preservation and book art."

Guild of Book Workers, The National Organization for all the Book Arts
http://palimpsest.stanford.edu/byorg/gbw/
"The Guild of Book Workers was founded in 1906 to establish and maintain a feeling of kinship and mutual interest among workers in the several hand book crafts... Its members hope to broaden public awareness of the hand book arts, to stimulate commissions of fine bindings, and to stress the need for sound book conservation and restoration."

International Creative Workshop (IMWe)
http://private.addcom.de/olaf/imwe/
"The International Creative Workshop (IMWe) is a unique cultural exchange programme for scouts from all over Europe."
   Workshop: BOOKBINDING
   http://private.addcom.de/olaf/imwe/book2000/bookbinding.pdf

Library Binding Institute
http://www.lbibinders.org/
"The Library Binding Institute (LBI) is a trade association of Commercial, Institutional and International Certified Library Binders and our suppliers. Its mission is to maintain and encourage support for the highest quality standards for Certified Library Binders and to promote their benefits to libraries."

Northeast Document Conservation Center (NEDCC)
http://www.nedcc.org/
The NEDCC "is the largest nonprofit, regional conservation center in the United States. Its mission is to improve the preservation programs of libraries, archives, museums, and other historical and cultural organizations; to provide the highest quality services to institutions that cannot afford in-house conservation facilities or that require specialized expertise; and to provide leadership to the preservation field."

Rare Book School (RBS)
http://www.virginia.edu/oldbooks/
RBS "is an independent, non-profit and tax-exempt institute supporting the study of the history of books and printing and related subjects."

Rare Books and Manuscripts Section, Association of College and Research Libraries, a division of the American Library Association
http://www.rbms.nd.edu/
"RBMS strives to represent and promote the interests of librarians who work with rare books, manuscripts, and other types of special collections."

Shaun B. Padgett Bookbinding: About Bookbinding
http://www.thebookbinder.com/html/aboutbb.htm
This is the site of an individual bookbinder and conservator. It contains some useful information.

A Simple Book Repair Manual
http://www.dartmouth.edu/~preserve/repair/repairindex.htm
"The web version of the Simple Book Repair Manual was created by members of Preservation Services, Dartmouth College Library."

Society of Bookbinders
http://www.societyofbookbinders.com/index.html
A society based in the United Kingdom, "the Society of Bookbinders is dedicated to traditional bookbinding and to the preservation and conservation of the printed and written word."

Bibliography

Ashman, John. *Bookbinding: A Beginner's Manual*. London: Charles and Adam Black, 1981.

Banister, Manly. *The Craft of Bookbinding*. New York: Dover, 1993.

Baumgartner, Peter. *Make Your Own Books and Boxes, Portfolios, Photograph Albums, and Decorative Papers*. Tunbridge Wells, UK: Search Press Ltd., 1996.

Burdett, Eric. *The Craft of Bookbinding: A Practical Handbook*. London: David and Charles, 1975.

Cockerell, Douglas. *Bookbinding and the Care of Books: A Handbook for Amateurs, Bookbinders and Librarians*. New York: Lyons and Burford, 1991.

Corderoy, John. *Bookbinding for Beginners*. New York: Watson Guptill Publications, 1967.

Darley, Lionel S. *Introduction to Bookbinding*. London: Faber and Faber, 1976. [Previously published as *Bookbinding Basics*. Toronto: Cole Publishing Company, Ltd., 1965.]

Diehl, Edith. *Bookbinding: Its Background and Technique*. New York: Hacker Art Books, 1979. [Reprint of the 1946 ed. published by Rinehart, New York; The Dover, New York, 1980 contains the two volumes bound as one.]

Greenfield, Jane. *ABC of Bookbinding: A Unique Glossary with over 700 Illustrations for Collectors and Librarians*. New Castle, DE: Oak Knoll Press, 1998.

Gross, Henry. *Simplified Bookbinding*. New York: Charles Scribner's and Sons, 1976.

Johnson, Arthur W. *The Practical Guide to Craft Bookbinding*. London: Thames and Hudson, 1985.

———— *The Repair of Cloth Bindings: A Manual.* New Castle, DE: Oak Knoll Press, 2002.

———— *The Thames and Hudson Manual of Bookbinding.* London: Thames and Hudson, 1978.

LaPlantz, Shereen. *The Art and Craft of Handmade Books.* New York: Lark Books, 2001.

Lhotka, Edward R. *ABC of Leather Bookbinding: An Illustrated Manual on Traditional Bookbinding.* New Castle, DE: Oak Knoll Press, 2000.

Marks, P. J. M. *The British Library Guide to Bookbinding: History and Techniques.* Toronto: University of Toronto Press, 1998.

Middleton, Bernard C. *A History of English Craft Bookbinding Technique.* New Castle, DE: Oak Knoll Press, 1996.

Middleton, Bernard C. *Recollections: A Life in Bookbinding.* New Castle, DE: Oak Knoll Press, 2000.

Middleton, Bernard C. *Restoration of Leather Bindings.* New Castle, DE: Oak Knoll Press, 1998. [Revised and expanded from the 1984 ed.]

Mitchell, John. *A Craftsman's Guide: An Introduction to Gold Finishing.* West Sussex, UK: The Standing Press, 1995.

———— *A Craftsman's Guide to Edge Decoration.* West Sussex, UK: The Standing Press, 1993.

Muir, David. *Binding and Repairing Books by Hand.* New York: Arco Publishing Co., 1978.

Reimer-Epp, Heidi and Reimer, Mary. *The Encyclopedia of Papermaking and Bookbinding: A Definitive Guide to Making, Embellishing, and Repairing Paper, Books, and Scrapbooks.* Philadelphia: Running Press, 2002.

Richmond, Pamela. *Bookbinding: A Manual of Techniques.* Ramsbury, Marlborough, Wiltshire: Crowood Press, 1995.

Vaughan, Alex J. *Modern Bookbinding.* London: Robert Hale, 1996.

Watson, Aldren A. *Hand Bookbinding: A Manual of Instruction.* New York: Dover, 1996.

Young, Laura S. *Bookbinding and Conservation by Hand: A Working Guide.* New Castle, DE: Oak Knoll Press, 1995. [Reprint of the 1981 ed. published by R.R. Bowker.]

Index

About the Author

Sharon McQueen is assistant professor in the School of Library & Information Science at the University of Kentucky. She has taught for the University of Wisconsin–Madison, School of Library and Information Studies; the University of Wisconsin–Milwaukee, School of Information Studies; and the University of Iowa, School of Library and Information Science. She holds a doctorate in library and information studies from UW–Madison and holds a doctoral minor in early childhood education, with an emphasis on emergent literacy. Sharon has presented extensively, including "Picture Books for Older Readers" for the University of Wisconsin–Madison's biennial children's literature conference; on "Defining Print Culture Studies for Youth" for the Center for the History of Print Culture in Modern America; and across North America on her dissertation, *The Story of "The Story of Ferdinand": The Creation of a Cultural Icon.* She has served on the planning committee of Library Research Seminar III and has been active in many professional organizations including the American Library Association's Association for Library Service to Children (ALSC) and the Association for Library and Information Science Education (ALISE). She was included in *Library Journal's* 2004 *Movers & Shakers* supplement. Librarianship is a second career for Sharon, who was formerly an actress and theater producer.

DATE DUE
